A Lakeland Paintbook

A LAKELAND PAINTBOOK

Wendy M. Stuart

Wendy M. Stuart

Hayloft Publishing Ltd, Kirkby Stephen, Cumbria

First published by Hayloft 2011

Hayloft Publishing Ltd, South Stainmore,
Kirkby Stephen, Cumbria, CA17 4DJ

tel: 017683 41568
email: books@hayloft.eu
web: www.hayloft.eu

ISBN 1 904524 84 2

CAP data for this title are available from the British Library

Designed, printed and bound in the EU

Papers used by Hayloft are natural, recyclable products made from wood grown in sustainable forests.
The manufacturing processes conform to the environmental regulations of the country of origin.

*For my dear friend John Crisp (1929-2009), recently departed to that higher place,
former Head of Towerwood Outdoor Education Centre, Windermere, (1968-1984),
without whose enthusiastic encouragement over the years I would never have explored
so many parts of the Lake District by foot or by boat.
It opened my eyes to the Lakeland I now love, and filled me for ever with the maxim
of 'can do if I try', an attitude that has equipped me for the rest of my life.*

A PREFACE FOR MY FRIEND

It is a warm midday in June that finds me listening intently to my friend Wendy Stuart, who begins the conversation in her now brightly lit kitchen, by telling me, when asked where it all began, how she could, "paint before she could even write! I had seven Victorian aunts, three of whom lived in our house, who placed high values upon such things as painting, piano music, and the arts in general, that all had to be mastered," she says over the rim of a coffee mug.

Now, many years on and having learnt to apply these values from her formative years she sees their wisdom, as indeed, she still takes her sketchbook on all of her many travels. "…I find that my painting helped me to add another dimension to those times, and essentially being able to return to those moments reminds me of those occasions much more informatively than say photographs or moving pictures could ever do - even though that might have been much more convenient at the time!"

Wendy is a remarkable lady. Having been educated at St Paul's Girls School in London where she came into contact with the likes of Victor Pasmore – a brilliant role model and eminent artist of his time, she went on to attend Twickenham Art College, then Chorley Teacher Training College, where she learnt her craft to begin teaching others.

She is an accomplished yachtswoman sailing single-handedly around parts of the United Kingdom, to the coasts of Europe and into the Atlantic Ocean. She has been a television presenter for the QVC channel and somehow manages to keep a garden that Capability Brown would be proud of! The rooms around where we are chatting are essentially a private gallery with paintings of all shapes and sizes shoehorned into spaces that happily seem to live side by side without issues of rank or stature.

However, it is the stack of A5 sketchbooks that live in the downstairs studio that are my favourites - as I thumb through each page I can not only see, but also 'feel' the time of day when they were crafted. I imagine myself looking over the artist's shoulder, watching her observing all of the nuances captured in those moments. Her tiny box of watercolours unpacked from a time worn spectacle case finds extra colours being creatively blended to suit the weather. The paper size - being so small, is quickly treated to a wash in seconds before the real action begins… until finally and with studied deliberation the fine detail is applied and the work is complete.

Overall, there is a continuous, harmonic signature in all of these simple but remarkable works that echo the quality of one who is skilled in their craft, who does not need anything more than perhaps two round sables (Nos. 2 and 7) a small screw-top jar of water and a place to sit for an hour or so.

In reluctantly closing this foreword, I am reminded of a term used by art critics that sometimes refers to a painting as being 'Painterly'. Slightly confusing in its intention: it nonetheless confirms the intention of the artist to pull the subject and the work together both visually and aesthetically. Van Gogh does this with his brush marks, Monet with his pallet; it is where the artist confides in the viewer's eye, that the subject is nothing if not faithfully described with feeling as well as skill.

Thinking of her words on the drive home I feel that a key aesthetic of Wendy's paintings comes not only from the style and content of their outcomes, but through a sense of paying tribute to nature in a way that perhaps some of us would like to observe, and later remember.

Charles Morton, BA (Hons), Lecturer in Fine Art, Runshaw College.

The Paintings in this Book

27. A carpet of unimpeded bluebells in the Duddon valley.
28. The dark waters of Stickle Tarn with Pavey Ark surrounding it in the Langdales.
29. Passing rain in the River Levens Estuary, south Cumbria.
30. Autumn colours of the two bridges in Grange in Borrowdale,
31. Poultry feeding on scattered corn in the farmyard.
32. Snowfall amongst the trees on Claife Heights, west of Windermere.
33. Sheep grazing in the bracken in Wrynose Bottom.
34. Early morning mist rising on Windermere.
35. The lone sentinel on Loughrigg Fell.
36. The Keswick plain shrouded in early mist.
37. The Miller Bridge over the River Rothay near Ambleside.
38. A calm evening on Ullswater, facing southern end.
39. Facing Staveley Head Fell and Potter Fell from Ings.
40. The Langdales viewed from Little Langdale and Blea Tarn Farm.
41. Wastwater, facing Great Gable and Scafell.
42. Conversation piece, "As I was saying..." Swaledale sheep.
43. Derwentwater seen from the western route, travelling north.
44. Fleetwith Pike from Dalehead above Honister Pass.
45. Ullswater, looking down from Keldas.
46. The Great Langdale valley and the Pikes.
47. Devoke Water on the north of Ulpha Fell.
48. Tarn Hows, north of Hawkshead.
49. A farm building above Longsleddale, eastern fells.
50. One of the old buildings in the well preserved village of Hawkshead.
51. Dawn fishing facing Narrow Moor and Derwent Fells.
52. Looking down on Yewtree Farm, near Coniston.
53. Mother and daughter sheltering in the Grizedale forest.
54. Morning mist lifting by Tower Wood jetties, Windermere.
55. Autumn view of Ashness Bridge on the route to Watendlath.
56. Rydal Cave, Loughrigg Fell, near Ambleside.
57. The River Eamont flowing into the northern end of Ullswater.

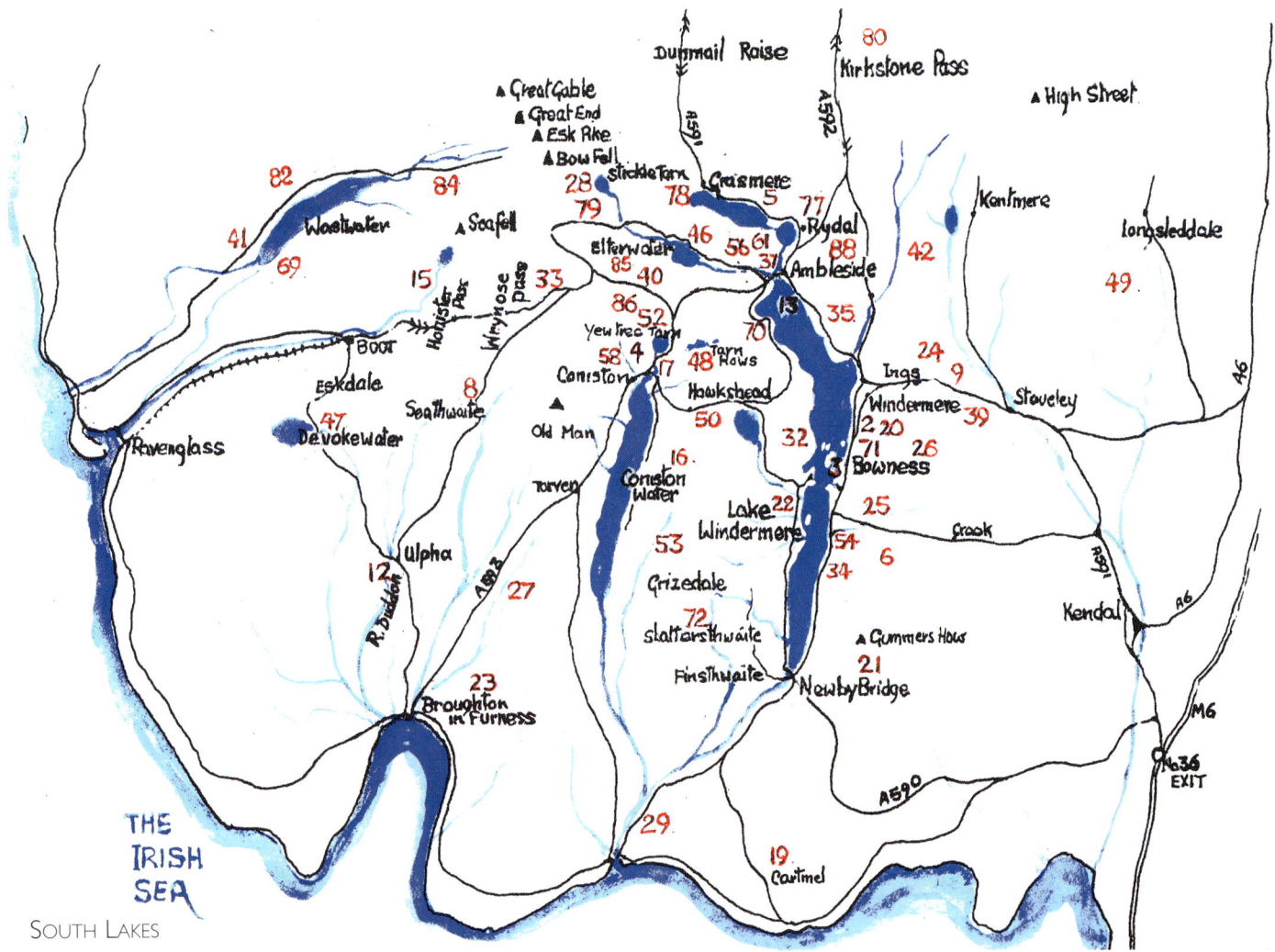

Dunmail Raise

Kirkstone Pass 80

High Street

▲ Great Gable
▲ Great End
▲ Esk Pike
▲ Bow Fell

Stickle Tarn

82   84

28   Grasmere

79   78   5

41   Rydal   77

Wastwater   ▲ Scafell   46   56 61   88

69   Elterwater   31   Ambleside

42

Kentmere

longsleddale

49

15   Hardknott Pass   33   85   40

Wrynose Pass   86   52   13   35

Boot   Yew Tree Tarn   70

8   58   4   17   48   Tarn Hows

Eskdale   Coniston   9

47   Seathwaite   Hawkshead   Ings

Devokewater   50   Windermere   39

Old Man   32   Staveley

Ravenglass   2 20

16   71   26

Torver   3   Bowness

Coniston   Water

25

Ulpha   22   54

12   Lake   Windermere   6   Crook

27   353   34

Grizedale   Kendal

72

Slattarsthwaite

▲ Gummers How

23   21

Broughton   Finsthwaite   Newby Bridge

in Furness

29

19

Cartmel

THE
IRISH
SEA

SOUTH LAKES

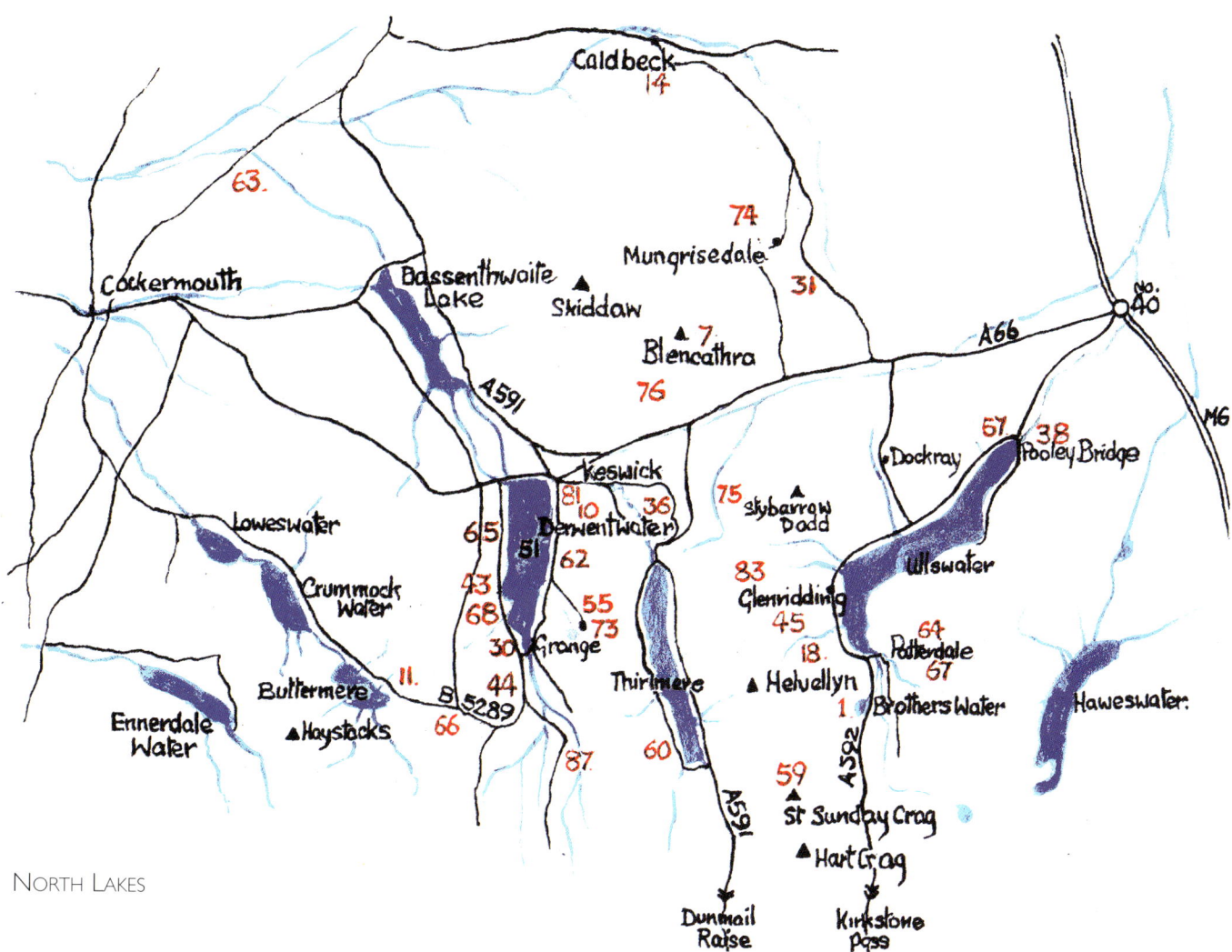

NORTH LAKES

INTRODUCTION

In forty years of rambling and sailing all over the Lake District, I was constantly amazed by the incredible views I saw in all directions, and often thought that I should be recording it, a feeling too strong to ignore. So I started carrying a small sketch book and paint-box in my pocket, sitting down on the spot to capture the view. If time or the weather did not allow, I would record the image soon afterwards with paint before the details of the memory faded, giving the results as much 'a feel' of a place as an accurate facsimile. This has been my usual pattern, and thus over time, I have accumulated a great many small sketchbooks created on my travels.

The watercolour sketches and pastels are not, and were never intended to be, works of art in any grand sense, but in the main they are the jottings merely to record the 'atmosphere' of the moment; the colours, shapes, moods, weather patterns, the joys and memories of well-loved haunts in the Lake District. Some sketches have been very brief, whilst others have taken me an hour or two. Sometimes I used the sketches for larger paintings at a later date, which gave me the pleasure of recreating the moods of that moment, in watercolours, oils or pastels.

Readers of this book who may be daunted by spending an hour or more under a tree with some paints, take heart – a page in an A5 sketchbook is such a small area to spoil, but if used, is much more likely to please you with a memory of some delightful sight, and produce a truer record of an emotion than a photograph or postcard could ever do. I rarely use a pencil, and if I need to draw, I prefer some 'dirty' paint-water and the tip of my brush for the purpose.

My pocket is small, so into a soft spectacles case I pack my paintbox, small screwtop bottle, two sable brushes, and a dual contact-lens container as water holder! Equipped in this way, I have stopped in many unlikely spots to record that fleeting weather pattern before it is lost, or the colour revealed on a hilltop by a shaft of sunlight through the clouds. I have used these hours of exploration and painting to clarify my mixed emotions, that have sometimes touched upon my life, so that when I gaze on these views, they remind me of those times with the saying that 'distance lends enchantment to the view' and now would not change a brushstroke of it.

Thus I have collected and stored many memories, areas of peaceful and hidden views, of wild and timeless countryside, with mountains, valleys, lakes and rivers, with forests, farms and fields, watered and weathered with the inevitability of the changing seasons. It is here with me to see in all its majesty and mystery; so I share a little of it now with you.

Wendy M Stuart, 2011

What we need is not the will to believe, but the wish to find out.
William Wordsworth

Travelling south towards the Kirkstone Pass, I stopped one evening in a gateway to admire a picturesque farm-house, and made this small painting of it. I was facing the small lake of Brothers Water in the Hartsop Valley. It lies at the northern end of the Kirkstone pass on the descent towards Patterdale

Dorothy Wordsworth strolled beside the lake on 16 April 1802, and in her diary remarked upon '...the boughs of the bare old trees, the simplicity of the mountains, and the exquisite beauty of the path... the gentle flowing of the stream, the glittering, lively lake, green fields without a living creature to be seen on them.'

This is a very small lake, and not well known, being shallow and full of reeds but at this point the view is colourful, especially when the water lilies bloom. Its name of Broad Water was changed in the nineteenth century after two brothers swimming there became entangled in the weeds and tragically drowned.

The village of Hartsop is to the south of this lake, where there are seventeenth century stone buildings and cottages. This name means "valley of the deer", for formerly the deer would have lived in the woodlands and lower areas of the fells. Brothers Water can be called one of the Lake District's smallest lakes or one of its largest tarns.

1. Brothers Water in Patterdale, looking towards the Kirkstone Pass from the north.

Brothers Water
Patterdale

The Lake District is, "A sort of national property in which every man has a right and interest who has an eye to perceive and a heart to enjoy."   William Wordsworth

Windermere is the largest lake, in two halves, in the Lake District National Park, upon which there are hundreds of sailing craft of all shapes and sizes. Many of them congregate in the north or south lake for racing at the weekends. Here I have recorded a race taking place in the north half on a bright summer's day, from the shore of Bowness.

Until the nineteenth century relatively wild, remote areas were seen as uncivilised and dangerous. However the Romantic poets such as Wordsworth found inspiration in the beauty of 'untamed' countryside, describing the Lake District as, "a sort of national property, in which every man has a right and an interest who has an eye to perceive and a heart to enjoy."

In the 1930s many leisure enthusiasts and conservationists such as the Ramblers' Association, the Youth Hostels Association and the Council for the Preservation of Rural England petitioned the government for access to, and protection of the countryside. After World War Two the movement towards creating National Parks gained momentum and finally did so with lasting effects, for the benefit of all.

Approximately 3.9 per cent of the National Park is owned by the Lake District National Park Authority. The rest is owned by other organisations such as the National Trust, Forest Enterprise and other private landowners. It is one of a family of fifteen National Parks.

2. Sailing on Windermere, looking north from the shores of Bowness.

Bowness Bay
Windermere.

Wendy M. Stuart.

Gardens are not made by singing "Oh, how beautiful," and sitting in the shade.
Rudyard Kipling

I anchored my boat off the shores of Belle Isle, the better to study this round house, previously seen only fleetingly as I sailed by from the north lake to the southern end, for I wanted to make a water sketch of it, so this time I made sure of carrying my paints with me. This I did, and finished off the fine details when I returned home, perhaps using a little imagination for the finished result!

The Round House was built for Thomas English, a wealthy Nottingham merchant in 1774 by John Plaw, a neo-classical architect on the original site of a Roman Villa built for the Governor, which became in 1250 the seat of the local Lord of the Manor. In 1698 Celia Fiennes, in her travel book recording her journeys through England, describes Sir Christopher Phillip's Manor as 'but a small mean place.' She continues:

"...it [Windermere] has many little hills or isles in it, one of a great bigness is 30 acres of ground on which is a house, the Gentleman that is Lord of the Manour lives in it Sir Christopher Phillips; he has a great command of the water, and of the villages thereabout and many privileges, he makes a Major or Bailiff of the place during life; it's but a small mean place, ...the Isle did not looke to be so bigg at the shore but takeing boate I went on it and found it as large and very good barley and oates and grass;"

It was bought, and also the Isle of Longholm on which it stood, by John Christian, a mine owner of West Cumberland, from the bankrupted Thomas English in 1781 for the sum of £1720. He bought it for his cousin Isabella Curwen, whom he later married, took her name and coat of arms and renamed the Island, Belle Isle in honour of her.

The Curwen descendants lived there until 1993, but a huge fire during the Christmas period of 1994 caused a great deal of damage to this strange house. This was eventually repaired and is now owned by the National Trust.

3. The Round House on Belle Isle, near Bowness, Windermere.

BELLE ISLE
WINDERMERE

W.M. STUART

Painting is by nature a luminous language.

Robert Delaunay

Having found the entrance to this slate mine at Tilberthwaite, near Coniston, I returned several times with my paints to make a series of studies of the curious rock formations. It is silent and eerie, except for the regular 'ping' of dripping water into the captive pools. With a strange luminous light filtering through the entrance to help me, I set to work speedily because of the fairly low but constant temperature. Having done my painting I started to research the place, and found out that it was previously named Horse Crag Quarry.

This was an adit (or entrance to an underground mine) driven into the side of the hill in 1849 by John Barret to connect with the extensive Tilberthwaite Copper mines, and as well as acting as drainage, allowed the passing of ore from higher levels. At the mouth was constructed the Penny Rigg Copper Mill, which was the copper-processing plant for this part of the mine. The adit is over 3,000 feet long, and still drains much of the workings.

In 1933 John Willie Shaw noticed that the adit had cut through an area of good slate about 300 feet from the surface. He continued working this until 1938 – for by then he had become too old. In 1989 George Tarr applied to operate Horse Crag as an underground closehead and continued to work Horse Crag more or less continually until it finally closed in 2001.

4. Tilberthwaite Slate Quarry, near Coniston.

OLD TILBERTHWAITE SLATE QUARRIES

Bald as the bare mountaintops are bald, with a baldness full of grandeur.

Matthew Arnold

Whilst travelling along the road from Ambleside to Rydal, I stopped in front of a packhorse bridge and perched on the low wall there. Looking towards the left, I studied the distant farmhouse, that I believe is called Oak Howe Farm, and the mountains behind with the patterns of light and shade in the autumn sunshine, that I recognised as the Langdale Pikes.

The striking autumn red tints of the brackens soon willed me into getting out paints and paper to record it, before I lost the sunshine effects, and the scene contrasted well with the light and dark greens of the grasses and the nearer knoll of trees.

5. Oak Howe Farm and Langdale Pikes.

LANGDALE PIKES
& OAK HOWE FARM.

Wendy M. Stuart.

I have been impressed with the urgency of doing.
Knowing is not enough, we must apply.
Being willing is not enough; we must do.   Leonardo da Vinci

The fleeting sunshine chasing clouds, and the onset of dusk produce dreamlike qualities - the sounds of roosting birds adds to the moment, almost suspended in time; then a total silence falls, as if by common consent by the settled birds.

This water sketch was completed when camping somewhere in the Great Tower Plantation, which is now owned and managed by the Scouting Association. The area is situated on the eastern side of Windermere, just south of the Beech Hill Hotel and is well known to me as an inspiration for many sketches, and is easily accessible on foot or by car.

6. Birds at dusk, Birkett House allotment, Great Tower Woods.

I listened, motionless and still; And, as I mounted up the hill,
The music in my heart I bore, long after it was heard no more.

William Wordsworth

Photographs of Sharp Edge were taken by a friend of mine on a dramatic climb, and not one that I would have undertaken. However the occasion filled me with admiration for his efforts, so I made a painting with watercolours and pastels, to create the feeling of coldness in the snow, as he had photographed it.

Blencathra is approached via Sharp Edge and I believe is the most technically difficult, where a head for heights is essential. This walk needs to be treated with respect, especially in severe winter weather. There have been some accidents, including fatalities on this route. It is reached via the A66 to Scales.

For some years the Ordnance Survey listed Blencathra with an alternative name of Saddleback, to liken it to the shape of the mountain seen from the east. Alfred Wainwright preferred to use the older Cumbric name Blencathra. It is likely that the name Blencathra came from the Cumbric word *blaen* (a bare hill top) and *cathrach* (a chair). Thus "the bare hill top shaped like a chair", describes in old cambric the shape of the hill, just as 'Saddleback' does.

There has been much mining activity beneath the slopes of Blencathra. The Threlkeld mine lies at the foot of Hallsfell. From 1879 to 1928 it was a profitable venture for the raising of lead and zinc ores and is believed to hold further reserves should the need arise.

7. Snow on Sharp Edge, Blencathra.

I thought of Thee, my partner and my guide,
As being pass'd away. - Vain sympathies!
For, backward, Duddon! as I cast my eyes,
I see what was, and is, and will abide;
Still glides the Stream, and shall for ever glide;
The Form remains, the Function never dies;
While we, the brave, the mighty, and the wise,
We Men, who in our morn of youth defied
The elements, must vanish; - be it so!
Enough, if something from our hands have power
To live, and act, and serve the future hour;
And if, as toward the silent tomb we go,
Through love, through hope, and faith's transcendent dower,
We feel that we are greater than we know.

William Wordsworth

I learned this poem when I was young, and it conjured up such a picturesque place for me, that I specifically travelled to the southern region of the Lakes to see for myself the place that had inspired Wordsworth. How true 'for ever glide' is to describe such a magical river – it is still there for me.

8. River Duddon flowing through the woods.

RIVER DUDDON

A work of art, which did not begin in emotion, is not art.

Paul Cezanne

Whilst walking with my dog at Ings, I passed along the gated road towards Crook. There are several unfenced small roads on the fells, one of which led me to this farm. With the mountains covered with heather behind, and the wind chasing the clouds across, this view had enough contrasts to spur me on to a quick sketch.

The fells around there are fenced off with many dry stone walls, and have gates across the roads, which are firmly fastened during the lambing season. There are several 'hog holes' built into these walls, allowing hogs (yearling sheep) to pass freely from one part of the heaf or pasture to another. One can walk from here to Windermere along the old small routes.

9. High Fairbank Farm near Ings, Staveley.

Farm at Ings, Staveley Windermere

Wendy M. Stuart

There are two things in the painter, the eye and the mind;
each of them should aid the other.

Paul Cezanne

I have visited the Castlerigg Stone Circle, north east of Derwentwater, several times and always with a feeling of wonder at the efforts that it must have taken to arrange them. Whatever the weather, they are always impressive, with sheep constantly acting as lawnmowers for the scene, in front of a backdrop of the fleeting colours of sky, with the shadows of drifting clouds that create patterns on the mountains.

There are 38 stones in a circle approximately 30 metres in diameter. Within the ring is a rectangle of a further ten standing stones. The tallest stone is 2.3 metres high. It was probably built around 3000BC - the beginning of the later Neolithic Period - and is one of the earliest stone circles in Britain. It is important in terms of megalithic astronomy and geometry, as the construction contains significant astronomical alignments.

Although its origins are unknown it is believed that it was used for ceremonial or religious purposes. There are some 50 stone circles in Cumbria, including some of the earliest stone circles in Britain.

10. Castlerigg Stone Circle, near Derwentwater.

CASTLERIGG KESWICK

Wendy M. Stuart

Travelling through Borrowdale and up to the Honister Pass, I eventually found a very peaceful lake at the bottom of the pass and paused on its shore to admire this discovery. The lake, Buttermere, had a surface so glasslike that every tree on the opposite shore, a row of pines, were faithfully depicted on its surface as a reverse replica, including the mountains behind them, High Crag and Haystacks. Here was a worthy spot to paint, so I set to work.

   The village of Buttermere is a small village that lies between Buttermere and Crummock Water, which were originally one post-glacial lake. The land between them has been created by the debris washed down from the surrounding hills. Buttermere is owned by The National Trust.

   The name Buttermere means 'the lake by the dairy pastures.' It is well known because of the story of Mary Robinson who lived there, the beautiful daughter of the Fish Hotel's landlord. She was known as the 'Beauty of Buttermere.' In 1802 she married Lieutenant-Colonel the Hon. Alexander Augustus Hope. Unfortunately for her, he was an imposter and a bigamist, who was hanged in Carlisle, not for bigamy but forgery! Her story was told recently by Sir Melvyn Bragg in *The Maid of Buttermere.*

11. Buttermere and the pine trees, with High Crag and Haystacks.

Buttermere & Haystacks.
Cumbria.

The flat appearance of the fells above Ulpha give rise to an interesting landscape of much foreground, distant hills and big skies. Birker is one of those areas. It is difficult to capture in paint the changing patterns and colours of such a scene, when a quick squall of rain passes overhead! For some years now I have been in the habit of carrying my umbrella, as well as donning the obligatory waterproofs, and thus equipped, have managed to avoid many of the disappointments of spoilt work

Water plays an important role in forming the character of Birker Fell for between the rocks and crevices flow many small streams, known as becks or gills in the local language. Many of the becks rise in one of the numerous bogs which occur in the area, the largest of which are White Moss, Sike Moss, Tewitt Moss and Foxbield Moss.

Ulpha is a small village in the Duddon Valley where a road leaves it to cross Birker Fell, meeting up with the valley of Eskdale. In the 2001 census the parish had a population of 159. The name Ulpha is believed to have originated with the meaning of 'hill frequented by wolves'. The name was derived from the Old Norse words *ulfr* meaning wolves and *haugr* meaning hill.

12. On the western fells above Ulpha.

Nature, with equal mind, Sees all her sons at play,
Sees man control the wind, the wind sweep man away.   Matthew Arnold

Sitting by Windermere at the north end and watching the many boats moored there, I can see the towering mountains beyond, offering the promise of further places to explore. I paint what I can see until the hourly Windermere ferry pulls in, and disgorges its many passengers, who melt away like snow into the area, and I am left once more with the peace of the boats and the ducks.

This is called Waterhead, and is closest the lake gets to Ambleside. Sailing up the lake from Bowness, it is fun to have a port of call to aim at, moor up, and take stock of the possibilities for the rest of the day. A walkable stroll into Ambleside widens the choices, for it is a very old market town, having had a charter granted in 1650 to hold agricultural markets for selling wool and other commodities for the farming community.

One famous building is Bridge House which spans over the Stock Ghyll stream, and is over 300 years old. It is claimed that it was used as a cool apple store, but is now owned by the National Trust. Rydal Mount, the home of William Wordsworth, is not far to walk, and from here also is Loughrigg Fell, the most accessible area for fell walking.

13. At Waterhead on Windermere, facing north towards the Langdales.

The Langdales at
Waterhead Windermere

Wendy M. Stuart

At one time I lived a few miles away from Caldbeck in Thursby, and had a mind to see the resting place of John Peel, the renowned fox hunter. Thus I came to be roaming this northern village, and rested for a while near some farm buildings. The wind was raw, and a few sheep had the same idea of sheltering from the weather. So I recorded this lonely group, to remind me of that cold day.

Caldbeck's name stems from the local river, the Cald Beck. This river has many tributaries, all of which provided in abundance water power for the industrial developments of the seventeenth and eighteenth centuries - woollen mills, bobbin mills, corn mills, a paper mill and a brewery. Many of these old buildings still exist in the village.

The first building in Caldbeck was thought to be a hospice for travellers that monks from Carlisle Priory built. In 1112, the first part of St Kentigern's Church, which is still the heart of the village, was built. Behind the church is St Mungo's well, a spring made holy by St. Kentigern. The churchyard is the resting place of two well known names, Mary Harrison, (the Beauty of Buttermere), and John Peel, the famous huntsman.

14. Sheep sheltering by old farm buildings near Caldbeck.

Works of imagination should be written in very plain language; the more purely imaginative they are the more necessary it is to be plain. Samuel T. Coleridge

Some years ago I was walking on the fells ascending Haystacks, accompanied by the skylarks, enjoying a very warm sultry day, when I came upon this lonely little tarn that had a still, mirror-like surface reflecting the heathers and the bracken. The colours in that moment of discovery were stunning to behold, and begged to be recorded in my paint book.

Innominate Tarn is a small lake in the northern Lake District and is, at 520 metres above sea level, near the summit of Haystacks. A tarn is a well known word in Cumbria, and I discover that it is derived from the Old Norse word *tjörn* meaning pond, and is commonly used for all small lakes in the mountainous areas of northern England.

It was formerly known as Loaf Tarn, because of small islands of peat in the tarn that somewhat resembled loaves of bread. I was told that because of the uncertainty of its name Wainwright christened it Innominate (meaning without a name) and this has subsequently stayed with it. Beside its shore is the location where Alfred Wainwright's ashes were scattered. He had expressed this wish in various of his books, including *Memoirs of a Fellwalker:*

'All I ask for, at the end, is a last long resting place by the side of Innominate Tarn, on Haystacks, where the water gently laps the gravelly shore and the heather blooms and Pillar and Gable keep unfailing watch. A quiet place, a lonely place. I shall go to it, for the last time, and be carried: someone who knew me in life will take me and empty me out of a little box and leave me there alone. And if you, dear reader, should get a bit of grit in your boot as you are crossing Haystacks in the years to come, please treat it with respect. It might be me.'
Alfred Wainwright

15. The isolation of the north western fells from Innominate Tarn.

INNOMATE TARN WITH
HAYSTACKS, CUMBRIA.

It is far better to draw what one now only sees in one's memory.
That is a transformation in which imagination collaborates with memory.　　Edgar Degas

Large numbers of sheep are reared on the hill farms and moorlands of Cumbria and the sheep population of Cumbria is around three million. This painting of the sheep foraging in the woods makes me realise how much the sheep 'tidy up' the countryside, and this one was too busy to take much notice of me.

The Herdwick, the Rough Fell and their close neighbour the Swaledale, have been bred and reared to thrive in the climate of the northern fells, and tough enough to withstand appalling weather, thus allowing the felltops to be farmed, and incidentally giving some areas a manicured look.

Local breeds have been shepherded for generation after generation, back to medieval times, to their own hill territory or 'heaf', to which they will always return. This means that these heafed sheep can be safely left on unfenced terrain and will not wander off their traditional patch. The lambs learn this behavior early from the ewes. Their legs are usually thicker and stronger than other breeds of sheep and they also have a special resistance to diseases, and parasites, like ticks - a characteristic taken advantage of by other sectors of the sheep farming industry to breed into their own sheep.

Many hill farms have 'fell rights' on which to pasture their sheep and cattle, turning loose several hundred sheep to roam the fells, and only rounding them up with sheepdogs, who know their own flocks, at special times for the management of the sheep.

16. Sheep foraging in the woods in autumn.

Direct observation of the luminous essence of nature is for me indispensable.

Robert Delaunay

How strong can be the midday sun, when walking in summer, creating contrasts of light and shade, and producing subtle shades of yellows, greens and browns, that mingle with the warm colours of the stone barn. I was hot - I was tired - I was hungry, having walked some way into the farmlands near Coniston, so I sat down on the verge to eat my lunch, watching and listening to the bees; and soon, not knowing, I fell asleep.

I woke up to find two sheep grazing the grass near my feet, quite unconcerned by this prostrate figure. I just had to paint this warm scene, and it reminds me to this day of those trusting sheep having their grassy lunch in such a measured way, accompanied by the constant humming of the insects going about their business.

If you should wander in that area you will find a very pretty valley to explore as well as the old village of Coniston; there you can find a working slate mine, the Ruskin Museum, and a beautiful house named Brantwood, the home of the poet John Ruskin. It is well worth a visit for all art lovers.

17. On a farm road near Yewtree Tarn, Coniston.

The best portion of a good man's life is his little, nameless, unremembered acts of kindness and of love.

William Wordsworth

Pooley Bridge was my starting point for this painting. I went to the ferry landing stage to admire the great mountains before me. The weather, ever changing, made patterns upon the mountain tops, shone shafts of sunlight through slits in the clouds and played dancing games on the surface of the lake. The scene became more rose coloured as the day advanced, darkening the foremost hills, like a dramatic set in a theatre.

Ullswater could well be the most beautiful of the English lakes. It is a narrow 'ribbon lake' which was formed after the last Ice Age, when a glacier scooped out the valley floor, then retreated, and the deepened section filled with water, becoming a lake. The surrounding mountains fashioned Ullswater into the shape of a long 'Z' with three distinct directions through the surrounding hills. For much of its length Ullswater forms the border between the ancient counties of Cumberland and Westmorland.

The origins are uncertain of the name Ullswater. Some say it comes from the name of a Nordic chief Ulf who ruled over the area; or a Saxon Lord of Greystoke called Ulphus whose land bordered the lake. The lake may have been named Ulf's Water in honour of either of these, or named after the Norse god Ullr.

18. Sunlight through the clouds over Hartsop Dodd and Helvellyn across Ullswater.

ULLSWATER

Fill the unforgiving minute with sixty seconds worth of distance run.   Rudyard Kipling

What excitement I felt whilst standing at the rails, as the powerful horses thundered past me within inches of my face. The grass was rough cut and churned up by the horses' swiftly moving hooves as they crowded together to gain advantage of the best route. This was no place to paint now, but rather to absorb the atmosphere, and record later with a swift water sketch, of three horses and a blur for the other participating runners.

Cartmel Racecourse is a small racecourse in the village of Cartmel, now in the county of Cumbria, but originally in Lancashire. Meetings are held on the May and August Bank Holidays. Although the racecourse is small, it is well known for having a four furlong run-in, the longest in Britain. For a small racecourse Cartmel attracts relatively huge crowds of 20 to 25,000.

The earliest written account of racing at Cartmel dates back to 1856. The course was supported by local landowners. Until World War II it was a very small course used primarily by amateur jockeys, but in the second half of the twentieth century the racing programme was expanded and became more professional. The course is situated on the Holker Estate.

19. The excitement of watching the horse racing at Cartmel, south Cumbria.

Cartmel Races
Cumbria

Wendy M. Reeves

Fine art is that in which the hand, the head, and the heart of man go together.

John Ruskin

This sketch was painted in the autumn, sitting on the jetty in Bowness Bay, watching the last of the sailing fraternity returning to their moorings after their day's sailing. Whenever one wishes to sail the length of Windermere, there is always the question of which way to circumnavigate the Islands that are scattered across the lake, and all have different names.

There are eighteen islands on Windermere. Many are called 'holme' after the local word for 'island', which originates from the old Norse language. Lady Holme, also known as St. Mary Holme, was named after the chapel that used to exist on the island, and Crow Holme was once used to kennel the local hounds of the Windermere Harriers, from whence they had to be rowed to the shore for exercise and hunting.

The Lilies are two islands that were named after the wild flowers that once grew upon them, and where in the eighteenth century tourists rowed to pick the flowers. The island of Hen Holme is used as a starting point for yacht races in the summer, and Silver Holme was the inspiration for Cormorant Island in Arthur Ransome's *Swallows and Amazons* books.

Belle Isle was previously named Long Holme, and also known as The Great Island, but was changed to Belle Isle in honour of the owner's wife, Isabella Curwen. It is the largest island on the lake, lies across Bowness Bay in the centre of Windermere and is one mile long. The unusual circular house was built in 1774. Wordsworth was deeply unimpressed, describing the house as looking like a tea canister in a shop window, or a pepper pot at other times.

20. The Lily Isles on Windermere in autumn, just north of Bowness Bay.

Windermere

Wendy M. Stuart

Some years ago I climbed Gummers Howe, a hill which overlooks the southern end of Lake Windermere, on the eastern shore of Windermere. I sat with my lunch and sketchbook, watching the sheep grazing with their newly born lambs, and realized that I could see almost to the Irish Sea! The view was amazing and worth recording in my little sketch book. Sheep strolled around me, taking no notice of my activities whilst I sat there quietly on my country mat, and studied the terrain before me.

It offered firstly views of the lake itself, then the Langdales, the Coniston fells and the fells above Ambleside, including the Fairfield Horseshoe, and definitely many more names which I did not know. I walked to the summit from the road at Astley's Plantation car park, which is over 200 metres above sea level, and therefore not so far from the summit.

The name 'how', comes from the Old Norse word *haugr*, and is a common local term for a hill or mound. Although a relatively small hill by the standards of the Lake District, it is the highest of the foothills in the area. It was my first experience of a panoramic view of the Lake District.

21. Looking down onto Windermere, facing west from Gummers Howe.

Windermere from
Brant Fell.
Cumbria

Wendy M Stewart

Who has seen the wind? Neither you nor I.
But when the trees bow down their heads, the wind is passing by.

Christina Rossetti

I found an interesting group of trees tucked into an old wall that created a real study of light and shade and harmonious colours. The country hereabouts offers a mixed variety of corners to paint, woodland and farmland in equal parts, with a scattering of old farmhouses and dwellings to study. I made several sketches here.

Through these woods runs Cunsey Beck which is one of several rivers and streams that replenish the lake of Windermere. Being just over two miles in length and generally slow flowing, it drains out of the end of Esthwaite Water, and finishes at the western shores of Windermere, near an island called Ling Holm.

Just before entering Windermere the beck passes through the deciduous trees of Cunsey Wood, and immediately before entering the lake, the beck is crossed by a footbridge which is part of a public footpath along a stretch of the western shore of Windermere.

22. Cunsey Woods, along the western shores of Windermere.

In the Woods,
Cumbria.

Wendy M. Stuart

The sky is the part of creation in which nature has done
For the sake of pleasing man.   John Ruskin

I was in the most southern point of Cumbria and at different places along the coast, when I made this sketch of the estuary flats, with this statuesque heron keeping its watch for a likely meal. My painting reminds me of the feel of this area, with a large sky, a flat watery foreground, and a hint of the Cumbrian mountains in the background.

   Just north of this is the River Leven, a short river in the county of Cumbria, falling within the historic boundaries of Lancashire until recently. I first encountered it when paddling a canoe down from Lake Windermere, which drains through from its southernmost point and flows for approximately eight miles into the northern reaches of Morecambe Bay. The upriver limit of tidal flow is close to the village of Haverthwaite. It was here that I went roaming along the coastal paths, watching also the birds who were making nests on the low flats amongst the reeds.

   The River Levens has one significant tributary, Rusland Pool, which drains a substantial part of Grizedale Forest and the Rusland Valley into the upper tidal section of the river. The Levens is a noted salmon river - at spawning time the fish can be seen jumping up the waterfalls at Backbarrow.

23. Heron fishing in the estuary near Haverthwaite, south Cumbria.

Heron Fishing

Wendy M. Stuart

Not where I breathe, but where I love, I live; not where I love, but where I am, I die.

Robert Southey

This is one of my favourite views of Ings with its heather covered mountains behind. Ings is a village in South Lakeland on the A591 road, to the east of Lake Windermere. This village is noted for its local pub, the Watermill Inn, which was awarded the Campaign for Real Ale 'Cumbria Pub of the Year' 2009, and the village church, St Anne, which was built in 1743. The chancel floor is of Italian Marble, which was funded by Robert Bateman, once a local, who became a wealthy merchant. He died aged 65 in 1743, by which time he was a prominent member of the British community of merchants living in Livorno. His reputation as the village's "boy made good" also spread throughout Westmorland. He even became one of the protagonists in Wordsworth's poem, *Michael.*

A school was endowed in the village in 1655. Historically within Westmorland, it became part of Cumbria in 1974. Near the village is the Craggy Plantation, which covers much of Spy Crag. This area was used in the 1990s for testing various measures to control the spread of North American grey squirrels into the native red squirrel habitats.

Gowan Beck meanders through the village of Ings. It is difficult to determine how the river got its name. In Scotland, gowan is the name for the common daisy or occasionally the buttercup, derived from the original form gollan which is the marsh marigold, made famous by Robert Burns in the poem *To a Mountain Daisy.*

William Wordsworth also uses the word gowan to refer to a common wayside flower and it is possible that the river got its name from the fact that it flows through many flower meadows on the valley floor. The area has been inhabited since around 4000BC when Celtic speaking Britons established farms. The Romans arrived in 90AD building a road that passed through where the village is now, linking Kendal to Galava (their main fort at Ambleside) and is still roughly followed today by the A591.

24. The village of Ings, near Staveley, Cumbria.

Wendy M. Stuart

INGS CHURCH, CUMBRIA.

Come forth into the light of things, let nature be your teacher.   William Wordsworth

The most dramatic pictures are usually executed unexpectedly, if one is at the right place at the right time. In the Lake District the weather and seasons play a large part in this scheme of things.

  Along the shore of Windermere are many beautiful trees of architectural stature which, when the leaves are fallen, are revealed magnificently during the winter. Added to this are the frosts and snows, clinging to the trunks, and highlighting the hidden contours, which immediately add contrast to the dark crevices within the trees.

  Behind these statuesque structures glows the sinking winter sunshine, filtering through the distant trees on the western shore, and reflecting the colours of an ever changing and fading pattern upon the water, until nightfall obliterates it all.

25. Low lying winter sunshine filtering across Lake Windermere, 1986.

Lake Windermere in Winter.

Wendy M. Steel.

I know that I shall meet my fate somewhere among the clouds above.

William Butler Yeats

I have sat and admired the views from the jetties of the Lake District Boat Club, from whence one can see clearly up the northern parts of the lake through the moored boats in Bowness Bay, and made several paintings at different times of the year. Autumn is the most colourful, showing up the white covered canvasses over the boats, that always reflect well in the stillness of the morning, or evening, when often there is no wind.

The first recorded yacht race was to be held on Windermere in 1818, using, as its land base, the inn at Ferry Nab. However, the race was not to be, for the wind was then, as it is now, very unpredictable! (Or in the case of 1818, absent). The hardy souls who wished to race were not put off and racing in an 'ad hoc' manner, continued for many years.

The Windermere Sailing Club was founded in 1860 and started to organise yacht racing on Windermere in a more formal manner with the construction of a 'one design' class, where all racing yachts had to conform to rather more accurate measurements. This resulted in the first 'Windermere' class racing yacht, having a waterline of 22 feet. Over the years, there has been continually a Windermere Class of different lengths, up to the present day, and only these boats are given moorings in Bowness Bay, in front of the Windermere Yacht Club.

26. Windermere Class Sailing boats moored up in Bowness Bay.

Bowness Bay
Windermere

Wendy M. Stuart

How does the Meadow flower its bloom unfold?
Because the lovely little flower is free
down to its root, and in that freedom bold.

William Wordsworth

Bluebells to me shout spring! Their dancing heads, waving with every breeze that passes, release their delicate perfume that hangs over the field of blue, intoxicating one's senses. This sight is a must for painting.

According to the light conditions, the blues vary from the deepest shades of ultramarine in the shadows for the newest buds, to the paler shades of the spent flowers, or in bright sunshine. They are always set off by the accompanying green sword-like leaves surrounding these woodland flowers, that are happiest in woodlands in the dappled shade.

I will not suggest which woods inspired this painting, but in my roaming in the southern area of the River Duddon valley in the spring, I spotted many beautiful bluebell woods, their colours ranging from the expected blue, to mauve and occasionally some pink.

27. A carpet of unimpeded bluebells in the Duddon Valley.

BLUEBELLS

WENDY M. STUART

No distance of place or lapse of time can lessen the friendship
Of those who are thoroughly persuaded of each other's worth.

Robert Southey

A few years ago I travelled with climbing friends to visit the Langdales and camped with them somewhere convenient for their serious climbing. They assured me that a climb to Stickle Tarn was worth the efforts, and as a painter they were right to encourage me. The tarn was a midnight blue as it sheltered below Pavey Ark, in the windless area of its shelter, while the rocks and boulders shone for a brief while in the sunshine.

It was a magnificent place to be. It lies in a dramatic location below the steep eastern face of Harrison Stickle (2,415 ft). The imposing crag of Pavey Ark (2,288 ft) towers above Stickle Tarn, a water filled corrie which has a depth of around 50 feet. The tarn was enlarged by the building of a stone dam in 1838 and is used to supply water for the inhabitants of Great Langdale.

Quoting Wainwright: "Pavey Ark is Langdale's biggest cliff. In an area where crags and precipices abound, here is the giant of them all, and scenically, it is the best." (*A Pictorial Guide to the Lakeland Fells: Book Three, The Central Fells,* A. Wainwright)

28. The dark waters of Stickle Tarn with Pavey Ark surrounding it in the Langdales.

STICKLE TARN
IN THE LANGDALES.

It is written on the arched sky; it looks out from every star.
It is the poetry of Nature; it is that which uplifts the spirit within us.   John Ruskin

When travelling down the river in a small boat or canoe, the view gained is low level, offering a perspective that is different from a more usual angle. The land appears flatter, with the skies being the most dominant feature. Winding my way silently through the tall autumn grasses and reeds in my small craft, I was more aware of the colourful skies and the effects left by a passing squall, than of the land through which I was passing. Autumn in the estuary has its own colour harmony of a restful nature, with the silence only broken by the calls of the marsh birds.

   I painted my impressions and memories of this area when I finally reached home again. I am reminded of that trip of long ago when I study my painting now which vividly recalls the moment when I became stuck in the reeds, which needed skilful manoeuvering to extricate my small boat.

   The River Levens is a short one, connecting Windermere to the sea, by passing Grenodd and into the estuary. It was probably the way that the Romans and then the Vikings took, to explore and colonize parts of the north of England, travelling up through Windermere. It was the way out to sea for the early mining industries, of gunpowder, minerals and slate, the quarrying industries being more extensive in this area then than now. These products were needed in other parts of the country so they were transported by boat, being a less expensive option than by land.

29. Passing rain in the River Levens estuary, south Cumbria.

PASSING RAIN

WENDY M. STUART

With an eye made quiet by the power of harmony, and the deep power of joy,
we see into the life of things.   William Wordsworth

Leaning against the wall facing Grange-over-Sands and admiring the double spanned bridge over the River Derwent, I hastily laid out my sketchbook and paints to capture the russet tones of this scene in the autumn sunshine. It was overshadowed by the hills behind, which were covered with bracken, and was perfectly mirrored in the still waters on the surface of the river.

Grange-in-Borrowdale is on the B5289, the road that connects Keswick to Buttermere via the Honister Pass, and is situated by the River Derwent, which flows north through Derwentwater. In medieval times the monks from Furness Abbey, owning land there, built an outlying farm (or Grange) which gave the village its name. The bridge was built in 1675.

30. Autumn colours of the two bridges in Grange in Borrowdale.

GRANGE IN BORROWDALE

WENDY M. STUART
2000

Blessed are they who see beautiful things in humble places,
where other people see nothing.   Camille Pissarro

I walked one day with a fell walking group who quickly disappeared from my view, as I was not a fast walker. It was raining intermittently, and one of the group came back to check on my progress, for during one heavy downpour I had ducked into a barn.

Knowing that I could not reasonably keep up with the enthusiasts I elected to wait within the curtilage of the farm for their eventual return, and thus happily used my time profitably with a painting of my surroundings, sitting in the doorway of a barn to keep warm and dry on that cold occasion.

This painting is evocative of many farmyards, where the poultry are able to roam freely around the yard, the tractor being parked handily for lunchtime, and the cattle watching vacantly, chewing the cud in their stalls. It is a timeless scene.

31. Poultry feeding on scattered corn in the farmyard.

Few have been taught to any purpose who have not been their own teachers.

Joshua Reynolds

The Lake District has more than its fair share of winter snows, falling well into the spring at times, and wherever you look when there has been a heavy fall of snow, the various trees become covered. It is very wind dependent as to whether the snow settles upon the branches in thick blankets or is flipped off with the vagaries of a stronger draught.

    Many people will say it is very picturesque, but it creates difficulties to walk through. The positive side, and to me the most interesting one, is to get out my paints and try to depict such a scene, in haste before the cold permeates my clothes. A limited palette will do, as can be seen in this water sketch done on the eastern side of Windermere above Claife Heights.

32. Snowfall amongst the trees on Claife Heights, west of Windermere.

The purest and most thoughtful minds are those which love colour the most.

John Ruskin

I travelled over this route from the Little Langdale Valley to reach the Duddon Valley, climbing a very steep road, not realising how great the gradient was. It is one of the steepest roads in England, with an incline up to one in three. When I reached the bottom of Wrynose, I decided to rest for a while, for driving on such a road is difficult.

Here I sat with my flask and surveyed the sheer magic of the view with bracken and yellow grasses vying with patches of green; a couple of belted Galloways strolled into my view whilst the sheep continued, as always, to amble around purposefully for their meal. I looked at an old tumbled down farm building, and noted the very stony beck, the River Duddon, running through the landscape, all of which were recorded in my watercolour.

The name Wrynose comes from 'pass of the stallion.' At the top of the Wrynose Pass is a stone marking the meeting point of the historic counties of Cumberland, Lancashire and Westmorland called the Three Shire Stone. The top of this pass has an altitude of 1281 feet. At the bottom of Wrynose is Fell Foot Farm, Grade II listed, and now owned by the National Trust. It was built in the seventeenth century.

33. Sheep grazing amongst the bracken in Wrynose Bottom.

WRYNOSE BOTTOM
FROM HARDKNOTT PASS

The half hour between waking and rising has all my life proved propitious to any task which was exercising my invention... It was always when I first opened my eyes that the desired ideas thronged upon me.   Sir Walter Scott

During the 1980s, I owned a Silhouette, a small sailing craft, in which I delighted to sail at the weekends, and moor up in a quiet area of Windermere. Providing the water depth was greater than three feet, (the draft of my boat being two feet and one inch) I had ample choice to find a peaceful corner in which to drop anchor, haul down my sails, and cook my evening meal, before retiring in my little bunk. The constant lapping of the water rocked the boat and accompanied the sounds of the ducks calling for their young.

By early morning as the mists were rising, the dawn chorus and water wildlife excelled themselves in activity, so now this was the time to do a painting of my 'quiet' mooring. The resident swans, who glide silently around the moored boats, have learned to tap on the sides of the craft to notify the owners of their presence, in the hopes of some titbits when they smell any kind of food or hear the rustle of wrappings, however quietly you operate.

Windermere is our largest lake, being eleven and a half miles long, approximately two miles wide at its maximum, and 219 feet deep at its greatest depth, and is known as a ribbon lake formed by glacial action thousands of years ago. Its name is said to come from the old Norse name, *Vinandr's* Lake, or a derivative of it. Boats are moored in most of the bays and inlets, so there is constant activity upon the water.

34. Early morning mist rising on Windermere.

Simplicity is the ultimate sophistication.

Leonardo da Vinci

An economy of paint and effort has produced this evocative painting, of an area that was my very first introduction to walking on the fells of Lakeland, and captured the essence of wide spaces and the feeling of the freedom to roam. Sitting on a boulder, it takes but a moment to put colour into the changing sky, then delineate the distant mountains with the morning light playing upon them, before studying the sparse foreground and placing my tree sapling, to pull the whole design together.

Loughrigg Fell needs no introduction to regular Lakeland wanderers, being in the central fells, between Ambleside, Grasmere and Langdale. It has roads on all sides, the height is a mere 1099 feet above sea level, and the easiest route is from the car park on the A591 between Grasmere and Rydal Water.

35. The lone sentinel on Loughrigg Fell.

Painting from nature is not copying the object; it is realizing one's sensations.

Paul Cezanne

Here I was on a hilltop, peering down at a snow covered Keswick, swathed in mist and bathed in a subtle pastel colour from the ascending sun. In gumboots I stood in the cold and the snow, my paints safely left behind at my lodging. I decided that the scene had to be recorded in watercolour, so this picture first started with a pencil sketch on the back of an envelope, shading in what I wished to depict, then soon rushed back for lunch, to where I was staying near Keswick.

By then the mists had risen, but my mind and memory was full of my morning sights, and I hastened to try recreating this scene, wetting the paper to flow in the colours in a misty fashion of this snowy scene. As Keswick was shrouded in mist, the only new layer to be added on top of the first was the nearest grey hill, the distant misty treetops and finally the grey walls of the silhouette of a farmhouse and trees. I lifted out with a damp paintbrush the snow covered mountain tops. And there you have it!

Under the mists lay the busy town of Keswick, one of the most northerly towns in Lakeland, that gained its wealth in the seventeenth century onwards by mining valuable minerals, and slate from the surrounding hills, and is now a thriving town with an ever growing population.

36. The Keswick plain shrouded in early mist.

STUART

It is not enough to know only your craft - you have to have feeling. Science is all very well, but for painters imagination is worth far more.   Edouard Manet

This painting is one of the few that was done with opaque 'school paint', (acrylic) but water paint nevertheless, therefore qualifies it to be in this collection, having been painted into my little sketchbook. In the 1970s I was camping with a small school party from my art department, at Tower Wood, when we found this delightful spot whilst walking from Ambleside to Rydal, having first sailed up Windermere to Waterhead. Along this route there are large beech trees on the left-hand side by the wall, and peering over, one can see the River Rothay down below.

   We climbed down to the riverbank to eat our packed lunches, after which we made sketches of the surrounding area and the old bridge. I had taken little bottles of school paint, everyone had small rucksack sized sketch pads with them, so soon there appeared an abundance of quaint bridges on these sketchpads. My bridge reminds me to this day of that far off occasion with pleasure, feeling the warmth of the sunshine in that secluded place.

   The name Rothay is said to come from the old Norse *Rathui* - the red one, and the Miller Bridge replaced another much older one that was swept away in severe floods in 1884. It was essential for daily use by the mill workforce, so the local mill owner set his gardeners to reconstruct it, which they did within one week using the local slate. It is now a Grade II listed building.

37. The Miller Bridge over the River Rothay near Ambleside.

Colour is my day-long obsession, joy and torment.   Claude Monet

This is one of two paintings of Ullswater from similar positions in this collection, but with vastly different weather conditions. When painting this sketch I am at the north end of the lake, facing south, but on this clear and windless evening the colours of the late sky are reflected in a dramatic way. With the sun shining upon the white hulls and masts, they show up well against the ever darkening foreground woods.

Along the western shore is the village of Howtown, where there is an active sailing club, evidence of which is the large number of boats moored around the lake. The other two main towns are Glenridding to the south, and Pooley Bridge at the northern end. On this lake, Donald Campbell set a water speed record of 202.32 mph in 1955, in his jet propelled hydroplane. Wordsworth was inspired by the daffodils growing along the shores of Ullswater to write his famous poem *Daffodils*:

I wandered lonely as a Cloud
That floats on high o'er Vales and Hills,
When all at once I saw a crowd
A host of dancing Daffodils;
Along the Lake, beneath the trees,
Ten thousand dancing in the breeze.

The waves beside them danced, but they
Outdid the sparkling waves in glee: -
A poet could not but be gay

In such a laughing company:
I gazed - and gazed - but little thought
What wealth the show to me had brought:

For oft when on my couch I lie
In vacant or in pensive mood,
They flash upon that inward eye
Which is the bliss of solitude,
And then my heart with pleasure fills,
And dances with the Daffodils.

38. A calm evening on Ullswater, facing southern end.

Art is not a study of positive reality. it is the seeking for ideal truth.

John Ruskin

I saw this view from the window of my lodging near Ings, and watched the progress of life in the surrounding fields. In this case, these were the flocks of sheep separated from their young which were ready for marketing, and put onto new grazing ready for the next season.

Facing Staveley Fell, and Potter Fell, I was particularly struck by the sunshine on the red hilltops that were emphasised by the threatening purple clouds coming up from behind the hill. Painting sheep in the distance is a matter of fooling the viewer into believing that what they see are sheep with gleaming white fleeces and black faces – in reality it is a lot of grey marks, with top white lines, black head-shaped dots and long grassy shadows in the right direction, and all arranged in a very random fashion!

Staveley is the nearest small town from here; it is four miles north west of Kendal, with the Rivers Kent and Gowan meeting, and it also boasts a stop on the railway line from Windermere to mainline Oxenholme. It used to have a cloth mill, a bobbin mill and a paper mill, the last of which is still operating. Staveley has been inhabited for a very long time, for the church of St. Margaret's was completed by 1388.

39. Facing Staveley Head Fell and Potter Fell from Ings.

Praise or blame has but a momentary effect on the man whose love of beauty in the abstract makes him a severe critic of his own works. John Keats

Travelling the length of the Langdale Valley to Dungeon Ghyll, I realised that the ever diminishing road continued to wind up into the hills, and onwards until I arrived at a smaller valley cradling a small tarn. As I was driving on a higher road I could look down on this scene, which surrounded farm buildings, and Blea Tarn.

Now I know the buildings as Blea Tarn Cottages, but then it was a working farm with much activity therein. I studied that autumn scene from my vantage point, and made a quick sketch, vowing to return on a warmer day for further painting - a vow that I never kept, but I still have my sketch with those sunlit Langdales as a backdrop to the cottage, to remind me of that trip.

The small tarn is 700 feet above sea level, and is partly sheltered by conifers. The word Blea for this tarn probably comes from the Old English *Blae* or the French *Bleu* - both meaning blue, and derivatives of this word have the same meanings in many languages.

40. The Langdales viewed from Little Langdale and Blea Tarn Farm.

Blea Tarn Farm.

Words, like nature, half reveal and half conceal the soul within.

Alfred Lord Tennyson

Sitting low on a boulder by the shore, this view offered an interesting slant to the scene, highlighting the autumn grasses and brackens contrasting well with the deep blues of the water. The rocks sat there teasing the ripples, and all I needed was some light red, ultramarine and raw sienna to fashion this view, with a hint of cerulean for the early morning sky. As the sun rose higher, the shadows deepened on Great Gable and Scafell, producing a dramatic effect.

The beautiful lake of Wastwater, which is in the western fells, is most easily reached by travelling to the A595 and making one's way eastwards into the Wasdale valley. It is approximately three miles long, is the deepest lake in England, and is 200 feet above sea level. Water from this lake, being very pure, has been used by Sellafield as a supply of fresh water.

This area was colonised by the Norse farmers of the ninth and tenth centuries, hence the name of the church at the head of the lake - St. Olaf's Church, which is one of the smallest in England.

Wordsworth described it as, "Long, stern and desolate," but although remote, it has great beauty.

41. Wastwater, facing Great Gable and Scafell.

WASTWATER WITH YEWBARROW, GT. GABLE, LINGMELL & SCAFELL

Thank goodness I was never sent to school;
it would have rubbed off some of my originality.

Beatrix Potter

These sheep appear to be having a serious conversation whilst feeding in the pasture. I have made several sketches over the years of various sheep, and this little sketch reminds me of how the sheep appear to congregate into little huddles! We used to keep sheep in North Cumbria many years ago, and every one had a personality of its own. No two sheep look alike, and farmers can tell one from another easily, as do their canny sheepdogs.

Although blackfaced, some have more, or less white or grey marks on their faces, and sometimes grey rings round their eyes. They are Swaledales, noted for their off white, but tough wool, and are most commonly seen in the uplands of Cumbria, Durham and Yorkshire.

The curly horns can be seen being used on the handles of sheep crooks, and made into other country artefacts. Originally in the seventeenth century, these sheep were known as Lintons, where they were bred tough enough for the harsh Scottish winters, and marketed around West Linton in Peebleshire.

42. Conversation piece: "As I was saying…" Lake District sheep.

"As I was saying......"
Blackface Tups.

When love and skill work together, expect a masterpiece.   John Ruskin

My painting of Derwentwater was an unexpected one; I see a view that cries out to be recorded! This was one such occasion when I pulled over to the side of the road, and rather hastily made my water sketch before the light altered in the colourful sky.

Travelling round the western route of Derwentwater, one sees a different perspective of this lake; the road is much higher, affording the sight of almost its entire length and spotting the many islands, unrealised from a shore position. The road is narrow with passing places for traffic, but the journey well worth the effort to view this, for me, an unaccustomed sight in the Lake District. From this vantage point also is seen the fells on the eastern side, through which I had travelled earlier.

I was travelling towards Swinside Stone Circle, (Sunkenkirk Circle) where there is an ancient stone circle of 90 feet in diameter, and still has 55 of the original 60 stones standing there. This circle dates back to the Bronze Age, and there is a legend about a church having been buried beneath the stones, hence the second name.

43. Derwentwater seen from the western route, travelling north.

*An architect should live as little in cities as a painter. Send him to our hills, and let him study
there what nature understands by a buttress, and what by a dome.*   John Ruskin

*This picture shows quite a dramatic scene of Fleetwith Pike from above the Honister Pass. It was painted with a
three layer system that I find quite useful. It might not be entirely accurate with all the details in place but it does
give the 'feel' of being high up above the pass, in bright sunlight and looking down upon Buttermere in the distance.*

*Three layers are often sufficient for painting a watercolour sketch; the first is a wash of the main shapes and
basic colours. When dried, the second is to put in the main large shadows or darker coloured shapes. The third, and
hopefully the last layer defines the details. In bad weather the first two sometimes get done, whilst the last awaits a
drier spot to finish it off!*

*The road that winds through the Honister Pass from Borrowdale to Buttermere, is extremely steep. One can rest
at the car park at the top, near the old slate quarries. There is evidence that this area was mined for slate in
Roman times, but certainly by the early 1800s there were substantial workings here. Green roofing slates of first
class quality have travelled far and wide. The old miners had to travel to their work daily from Seatoller, Stonethwaite
and Rossthwaite for very little pay, and the vagaries of war and hard times have closed it down several times. It was
reopened again in 1997, and has since become a thriving tourist attraction, whilst still working a smaller amount of
slate. Here is the greatest amount of rain in England, some 100 inches per year!*

44. Fleetwith Pike from Dalehead above Honister Pass.

Honister Pass

Every picture shows a spot with which the artist has fallen in love.

Alfred Sisley

Looking down from a great height upon a place gives it a whole new perspective. I had travelled through Glenridding a few times exploring the perimeter of Ullswater, then decided to view it from a higher level.

The path, starting through Glenridding drew me ever upwards until I reached this magnificent view of the lower reaches of Ullswater, standing on Keldas amongst a few pines. The presence of brackens and ochre coloured grassland lent a contrast to the heather covered mountains in the distance. The water, being very deep, picked up on midnight shades of blue from the cloudless sky. This was truly a colourful spot, and I happily set to work to record this kaleidoscope of colours before they inevitably changed.

Ullswater is seven and a half miles long, having three towns on its shores, the southernmost one being Glenridding, and from here the steamers sail regularly northwards to Howtown and Pooley Bridge. Now a great tourist attraction, this area produced lead ore in the 1650s, which was extensively mined until it eventually became uneconomic and the mines were closed down.

45. Ullswater, looking down from Keldas.

ullswater
from Keldas

Everything is beautiful, and all that matters is to be able to interpret.

Camille Pissarro

The Langdale Valley is the very first area that I explored as a seventeen-year-old, creating a meticulous oil painting of the scene, and taking at least a week over its creation. Later on as a busy adult on holiday, I made this sketch in my little book to remind me of that visit. Evening summer sunshine glows and with lengthening shadows, it creates for me an enduring Lakeland pastoral scene.

This area is reached by driving from Ambleside, and wending one's way up the valley along a very narrow road, then reaching the Dungeon Ghyll, a well known mountain stream at the head of the valley that cascades down the mountain, in a very impressive fashion with beautiful waterfalls. At that point, climbing up beside these falls, one sets off to reach Stickle Tarn above. Along this road through the valley can be seen the unmistakable mountains of Langdale Pikes and Pike of Stickle, and I have depicted them here.

The Old Dungeon Ghyll inn, situated at the foot of the gushing stream is the focal point for everyone who enjoys that area, be it for painting, rambling or climbing!

46. The Great Langdale valley and the Pikes.

LANGDALE PIKES.

This water sketch reminds me of a wet trudge through some very boggy land, but the weather and warmth improved as the day advanced. By the time I reached the water's edge, I was really ready for sitting on my country mat and raising my energy levels, by eagerly eating my lunch. The colours were dramatic, and another water sketch had to be done.

    This area is devoid of trees, high up on Birker Fell, but the largest tarn sits here and is called Devoke Water. It is almost a mile long, 46 feet deep and its altitude is 770 feet. It can be reached via a bridle track from the fell road connecting Ulpha, Eskdale and Boot. The only signs of human activity are a two-storey stone boat-house-cum-refuge and a ruined stable. Water from the tarn eventually plunges over rocks down a 26 foot cascade, towards the River Esk.

    It is believed that the name Devoke comes from the old English term *dubaco*, which means the dark one, but in the thirteenth century Devoke Water was named Dudockis Terne. These windswept fells were forested with oak trees 3000 years ago, but sheep grazing took over as the trees declined, and it has been discovered that a large Bronze Age community once lived here. There are brown trout here, which are said to be the most radioactive fish in England!

47. Devoke Water on the north of Ulpha Fell.

DEVOKE WATER.

Where the spirit does not work with the hand, there is no art.

Leonardo da Vinci

I have made many visits to this beautiful lake, and found it to be a great source of inspiration for painting, especially whilst my four boys were young and played along the shore. It is to be found a short distance north west of Hawkshead. This watercolour sketch was done before the major alterations took place, making it more user friendly to the public.

The stream which joined the tarns was dammed in the nineteenth century. It is now a man made lake, created from three smaller tarns, known as High Tarn, Low Tarn and Middle Tarn which occupied an area of marshland. Beatrix Potter bought the Monk Coniston estate, which included the tarn, for £15,000 from James Garth Marshall in 1929. She sold half of the estate to the National Trust, and bequeathed the other half to the Trust in her will. They have maintained the tarn since then.

In 1965 Tarn Hows was designated a Site of Special Scientific Interest, and the wildlife there includes red squirrels, now a dwindling population in Britain. The word tarn is derived from the Old Norse word *tjorn* meaning teardrop, and 'how' is Norse for hill.

48. Tarn Hows, north of Hawkshead.

Tarn Hows.

Come Fairies, take me out of this dull world, for I would ride with you
upon the wind, and dance up on the mountains like a flame!

William Butler Yeats

I walked up the valley of Longsleddale, and far up onto the fells without being aware of the place names, but only of whence I had started. The gathering clouds and the autumn sunshine showed up the track in the yellowed grasses, and the fells in the distance. There was a building ahead, which I took to be a shepherd's refuge, and here I recorded what I had seen before retracing my steps. The heavens opened and I, with waterproofs and umbrella, hastened down the valley again before it was totally dark. So now I have my quickly painted sketch to remind me of that occasion, and afterwards I took time to research a little of the area.

Longsleddale is a valley of South Lakeland. It includes the hamlet of Sadgill, which has a population of only 73. It is bounded to the west by Kentmere Pike and Shipman Knotts, and a part of the Kentmere Horseshoe, and to the east by Sleddale Fell. The River Sprint starts on these fells, and flows south through the valley before joining the River Kent, the north end of the town of Kendal.

This area was the inspiration behind the fictional Greendale village, the setting of the *Postman Pat* books and the television series for children, based on the books.

49. A farm building above Longsleddale, eastern fells.

Across the Moors   Wendy M. Stuart

Time stays long enough for anyone who will use it.

Leonardo da Vinci

I have made a few drawings and paintings of Hawkshead over the years, but this sketch shows the ancient character of the buildings and the haphazard nature of the arrangements of the narrow cobbled streets. You can sit in any corner (no traffic!) to view many different aspects for studying or painting, then pop into a little teashop for sustenance.

Hawkshead is a pretty village set in the beautiful vale of Esthwaite, and is an ancient township, that has flourished since Norse times, belonging to Furness Abbey until the twelfth century. The monks built and owned Hawkshead Hall, just outside the village, but the courthouse is all that remains of that building. It was a prosperous mediaeval wool town.

After the dissolution of the monasteries in 1537, Hawkshead grew as a market town, with many buildings dating from the seventeenth century to later buildings such as the grammar school (1855) which the poet William Wordsworth attended and is now a museum housing the history of Hawkshead. The Church of St Michael and All Angels stands high in the centre of the village, with fine views of Esthwaite Water, Claife Heights, Latterbarrow, Helvellyn and the Langdales. Grizedale forest is to the south.

50. One of the old buildings in the well preserved village of Hawkshead.

There are no lines in nature, only areas of colour, one against another.   Edouard Manet

This painting has a visually peaceful and tranquil aura for the location, colours and subject matter, and lends itself to restful thoughts so early in the morning before the mists have fully cleared. A very limited range of colour has added to the calm scene. The early morning fishermen on Derwentwater row back and forth peacefully with their rods, for perch, roach and trout, which are present in large numbers, but the famed char are not, because this lake is too shallow for them.

   Unlike most of the larger lakes, Derwentwater is relatively shallow, and has an average depth of just under twenty feet. During the summer months most of the fishing is concentrated around the shallower bays, where fly fishing can produce good bags. Come winter and the colder weather, the fish move out into the main body of the lake. It is also the first lake to freeze over in severe weather. Boat fishing is a preferred option then for regular visitors, and launching and hire facilities can be found for this purpose round the lake.

   Keswick is situated at the north end of Derwentwater, and from there I walked around the lake to look for good painting locations. It really is a beautiful place. Approximately three miles long, it has four islands one of which is occupied by tenants of the National Trust in the eighteenth century building, Derwent Island House. There are regular launches to take trips around the lake for spotting many of these hidden gems.

51. Dawn fishing facing Narrow Moor and Derwent Fells.

Thank God I have the Seeing Eye, that is to say, as I lie in bed I can walk step by step on the fells and rough land, seeing every stone and flower and patch of bog and cotton grass, where my old legs will never take me again.   Beatrix Potter

I had a very comfortable few days stay at Yew Tree Farm, and soaked in the amazing views around me. This area is a paradise for painters, for the farm sits at the bottom of a narrow valley aiming towards the mountains above Coniston. Overlooked by the purple heather crags, amongst the surrounding woods, are fields for herds of Belted Galloway cattle and flocks of the Herdwick sheep that Beatrix Potter worked so hard to protect. A hardy, grey-fleeced breed, with their large white heads, and knowing expressions they populate much of the Lake District, being well suited to the harsh, wet climate.

Beatrix Potter bought Yew Tree Farm in 1930. She advised the tenant farmers to augment their wages by setting up a tea room to serve passing hikers, providing the furniture and ornaments to help furnish it suitably from her own collection, and watercolours of Lakeland scenes, a cabinet of china, and a display of letters from Wordsworth, Ruskin and Southey. Yew Tree Farm doubled as Hill Top in the film *Miss Potter*, which was altered believably to fit its role.

52. Looking down on Yewtree Farm, near Coniston.

Yew Tree Farm
Coniston

There are no strangers here - only friends you haven't yet met.   William Butler Yeats.

My painting was done, while this Rough Fell ewe was guarding her offspring, and quite content to stay still in the sunshine. This one was on the edge of the forest, where sheep are not usually to be found within the curteledge of the trees as they are usually grazing on pastures or the fells. They can survive on very poor upland areas with scarcely any grass. These sheep were bred originally in the area of parts of old Westmorland, the West Riding of Yorkshire and Cumberland, and the old alternative name for them was Kendal Roughs.

    Rough Fell sheep have horns, black and white patchy faces, and thick, long, tough wool, which is nearly white, and often used in carpet manufacture. The horns of these sheep can be a real boon for the farmers when handling their livestock, to use as a couple of handles! Also, their legs are much thicker and sturdier, to cope with their hilly lifestyle than the lowland breeds of sheep. Some ewes have only one lamb, which tends to be much bigger, thus not having to vie for attention and milk from its mother.

53. Sheltering in Grizedale Forest.

SHELTER IN
GRIZEDALE FOREST

Silence is more musical than any song.   Christina Rossetti

This drawing was done as a 'before breakfast' study, prior to the heat of the day, or the sun fully up, with no wind or moving boat to shatter the flat calm of the water's surface on Windermere. Drawn with only five pastels in my pocket and a piece of charcoal, it evokes the peaceful moment before the business of the day erupts into the movements, sights and sounds of boats, ducks, birds, and people, especially at the busy outdoor education centre of Tower Wood where I made my sketch!

   Tower Wood was originally an Edwardian Lake District family house. The oldest part of the building dates back to the seventeenth century but most of the house was converted in the early 1900s to improve the accommodation, then eventually bought by the Lancashire Education Authority in the mid-1900s when it was changed yet again to make it fit for their purpose. It is situated on the lower eastern side of Windermere on the A592.

54. Morning mist lifting by Tower Wood jetties, Windermere.

For an Impressionist to paint from nature
is not to paint the subject, but to realize sensations.

Paul Cezanne

I sat on a fairly flat rock on a warm sunny afternoon and gazed down upon Ashness Bridge listening to the continuous flow of the stream beneath it. I could see far below me a panoramic view of Derwentwater and the fainter hills beyond. The trees had turned to russet reds and browns deeper than that of the brackens. This was a picture to be done in my little sketchbook before the afternoon warmth failed.

Ashness Bridge is so famous a landmark in Cumbria, that it needs little introduction. But, for those people who are wondering where the spot lies, it is to be found up a very minor road to Watendlath, a turning off the B5289 that lies alongside Derwentwater. It is a traditional stone bridge on the single track road, spanning the rushing torrents of the Barrow Beck. It is really a painter's paradise with the autumn tints being truly magnificent.

55. Autumn view of Ashness Bridge on the route to Watendlath.

Ashness Bridge

From near Rydal Water, I went rambling up the hills to Loughrigg Fell, which is covered by humps and hollows formed by ancient volcanic rocks, and facing me I found a dramatic entrance to a cave. I explored inside and out, then sat down to make a painting. Because of the recent rain, the water prevented me entering too far, but I was happy to explore the shapes and colours of the roof rocks and the reflections in the greenish water.

Rydal Cave is actually a man-made cavern, which was formerly known as Loughrigg Quarry. The cave has been hollowed out of a rocky outcrop which overlooks the picturesque lake. It used to be a busy working quarry about 200 years ago supplying roofing slate of excellent quality to the surrounding villages. The cave forms a mini-ampitheatre, the entrance being framed by jutting, angular rocks, which encloses a pool supporting small fish and insect life.

Rydal Water is one of the smallest lakes at just three quarters of a mile in length and one quarter of a mile wide, with a depth of 55 feet, but it is very popular, partly because of its Wordsworth connections.

56. Rydal Cave, Loughrigg Fell, near Ambleside.

RYDAL CAVE
LOUGHRIGG FELL.

All great and beautiful work has come of first gazing without shrinking into the darkness.
John Ruskin

This part of Ullswater does not often draw attention to itself, for I saw this particular view whilst leaning on the Pooley Bridge that crosses the River Eamont as it flows away from Ullswater, travelling north towards Penrith. The evening scene appealed to me as I studied the distant hills to the south, and watched the slow escape of the lake water as it meandered in curves, looking for its exit to the north, so I proceeded to record this little scene, before I departed to my caravan, doing another from memory there.

The bridge was built in the sixteenth century over a pool, now gone, hence the name of this northern small town on the lakeside. Pooley Bridge used to be a small fishing and farming community. The area still has a supply of trout, salmon and a freshwater herring named the schelly. From near this point, the Ullswater Steamers also depart making trips along the seven mile lake to Howtown and Glenridding at the southern end.

57. The River Eamont flowing into the northern end of Ullswater.

RIVER EAMONT & LAKE ULLSWATER

On the road from Ambleside to Coniston, close to the roadside you will find a peaceful small tarn that is worth pondering over. I made a pastel drawing of it, being surprised when I studied it further, by the deep turquoise shades needed to depict it, realizing that the bed of this lake was made from some reflective clay of a kind not necessarily local to the area.

It has an unusual history which might be the answer to this curious phenomenon. The area was a miniature tarn on the course of Yewdale Beck, sometimes drying out in hot weather. A local landowner, fond of trout fishing, decided to dam the tarn in the 1930s, to a depth of at least ten feet. The materials used for this undertaking could have been a kind of clay that would have given the lake its strange colours.

Yewtree Tarn was then stocked liberally with trout, for the benefit of his sport, and no doubt the local fishermen. In 2010, during the severe drought, volunteers removed many of the larger fish to a nearby pond for safekeeping, only restocking the tarn when safe to do so

58. The path round Yewtree Tarn, by the road to Coniston.

Take, if you must, this little bag of dreams, Unloose the cord,
and they will wrap you round.   William Butler Yeats

When my climbing friends returned from a trip up St Sunday Crag, they were very elated by their efforts, and showed me their photographs. I realised that this was a climb too far for me. One asked me to make a painting of the view, so I made a water colour sketch from his shot into my little book, to use for reference when I returned home. Subsequently I completed a larger painting for my friend, to whom I was also teaching watercolour techniques. His group said that the distant views over Grisedale were magnificent, the mistiness of the valley showing up a couple of large black birds wheeling above them, riding the thermals.

   Grisedale is reached by starting off in Patterdale, and thence into the hills, leaving the lower end of Ullswater far below. St Sunday Crag is one of several on the Pinnacle Ridge, and is a challenging climb for those who aspire to reach it.

59. Grisedale and St. Sunday Crag on Pinnacle Ridge.

ST SUNDAY CRAG - PINNACLE RIDGE
OVERLOOKING ULLSWATER

WENDY M. STUART

Invention, strictly speaking, is little more than a new combination of those images, which have been previously gathered and deposited in the memory. Sir Joshua Reynolds

Walking on the western side of Thirlmere in spring, I was struck by the total absence of movement, from air or water, and the reflections in the water accurately mirrored the scene ahead. The day became warmer, but the cold snows still looked deep on Helvellyn. I reached for my paints to capture the varying shades of blues and mauves, which contrasted well with the blue-greens of the spruces, and pale greens of the early spring growth.

It is now possible to see more of the surrounding areas of Thirlmere, for once it was very restricted land, but travelling on the smaller route round the western side is very picturesque. This is not strictly a lake, rather a reservoir, the dam being built in 1894 by the Manchester Corporation for augmenting their supply of water. The dam raised the water level sufficiently to drown two previous lakes, Leathes Water and Wythburn Water, and also the hamlets of Armboth and Wythburn, creating this lake, three and a half miles long and 158 feet deep.

60. Thirlmere, with Wythburn and Helvellyn, early winter's morning.

THIRLMERE
EARLY MORNING

An art, which isn't based on feeling, isn't an art at all.   Paul Cezanne

Winters in the Lake District can be regularly so severe that traffic movements come to a halt for a while. But it is also one of the most beautiful times when deep snow has fallen, to look at this strange new world laying there for only a very limited period.

This sight of Rydal captured my imagination for the range of blues and pinks it offered as a painting, so I painted the background first with the paler range of colours, then needed a dramatic foreground to lend distance to the view. The stillness in this windless place allowed the snow to lay along the branches undisturbed, so it has been over painted with white gouache along the near branches to achieve this effect.

Rydal Water is only three quarters of a mile long, with a depth of 55 feet, and is so still with no boating traffic, that in the winter it soon freezes over. The fishermen like it, for there are plenty of pike, roach, perch and eels to catch. Nicknamed 'Skaters Pond,' and once referred to as Rothaymere, it lies upon the course of the River Rothay, and is mentioned in historical documents in 1274 as Ridale and Rydale. This name is derived from the Old Norse meaning 'valley where rye is grown.' At the Grasmere end of the lake White Moss House stands, in which until the 1930s, the descendants of William Wordsworth used to live, for he bought it for his son Willie.

61. Winter through the trees on Rydal Water.

No art can be noble which is incapable of expressing thought, and no art is capable of expressing thought, which does not change. John Ruskin

This pastel drawing was created on pale brown pastel paper with only five colours involved; ultramarine, cerulean, white, brown and black charcoal. A crisp, cold, calm morning produces this kind of view, and I wished to record this effect in the very early morning light before such peace was dispelled. A fixative spray was the only extra item needed to make the drawing more permanent, so Derwentwater, with the majestic snow capped fells was saved, to take home without damage.

When sketching along the shores of a lake, the perspective of the view is vastly different to that of a camera. One emphasises what is important to one's own vision, whereas the camera 'flattens' the whole scene. Thus the distant fells, the Jaws of Borrowdale and Catbells, are the focal point here, with their mirror images, and Friars Crag is less important, though visible, on the right hand side, and seen from further along the shore.

Friars Crag itself, is a beautiful vantage point for surveying Derwentwater, and has a bench placed there upon which to rest. Its name comes from the fact that the Friars set off from this point to row across to Saint Herbert on his island with his supplies. He was a hermit, a friend of St. Cuthbert of Lindisfarne, both of whom died on the same day 13 April 687AD.

62. Derwentwater reflections, showing Friars Crag.

Reflections

Colour is a matter of taste and of sensitivity.　　　　　Edouard Manet

The architectural shapes of the buildings, the trees, and the blocks of definite areas of colour drew my eye to stop and look carefully at this scene. I was in the car, travelling in the northern part of the Lake District, and did not have my usual paintbox with me. However, nothing daunted, I used some other paints in the car that were unfamiliar to me, and proceeded to record the scene. It finished up with simple blocks of colour, reminiscent of a tapestry layout, but still true to the view, and the final result was surprising, but pleasing.

　　Over the years, I have driven many miles in the north west, taking in what I see almost unconsciously, sometimes stopping to record, thus many views are stored away in my memory without knowing afterwards where they were. I have sometimes retraced my steps to find the name of a place without success, leaving my sketches as a reminder of having been and seen such a view.

63.　Contrasting trees by a roadside farm in Cumbria.

In painting you must give the idea of the true by means of the false.   Edgar Degas

Some years ago I went to visit my cousin, Margaret Crosby and her husband who lived remotely at Crookabeck in Patterdale. Sadly they are gone as time passes, but my memories live on in the paintings that I produced then. One Easter, intending a short visit of four days, I found myself stranded there, with deep snow cutting off my return travel for nearly two weeks. It was a beautiful place to be caught out with the vagaries of the weather, so I made the most of that extra time by making many paintings and sketches, two of which are here in this collection. As the snow continued to fall, I sat by the window watching how quickly the large flakes could obliterate the barn and small beech tree, with Hartsop Dodd in the background. The silence and tranquillity haunts me yet.

    Life continues to flourish there, as Crookabeck is still a working farm, run by Margaret's daughter Mary Bell, and now famous for its Angora goats and Helvellyn Herdwick sheep. You find this interesting place by travelling over the Kirkstone Pass, turning right over a bridge as you enter Patterdale and following the small road towards Hartsop, a little hamlet, by the Pasture Beck, that is a cluster of seventeenth century listed buildings with many features, such as spinning galleries and chimneys of that period.

64. The barn at Crookabeck Farm, Patterdale.

We build statues out of snow, and weep to see them melt.   Sir Walter Scott

On a bright winter's day when the air is cold and clear, the colours of the countryside are highlighted and enhanced by the reflective snow. All this is not so pronounced when it is warmer and possibly mistier, masking some of the more subtle areas to look at, but the intensity of these positive colours in winter are just waiting to be used in a painting! The cerulean skies, mauve mountains and deep green foliage complement each other well, and the snow surrounding the sheep only require a little judicious placing of blue-grey shadows and yellow tufted grasses, to make the picture complete.

    The Skelgill Farm buildings were originally built in the thirteenth century, but the house is mainly Georgian. It stands looking north west towards Rowling End and Causey Pike, with Outerside and Grisedale Pike in the distance, and is near Swinside on the western side of Derwentwater. Now the buildings are used for tourist accommodation.

65. Skelgill Farm, Swinside, near Derwentwater.

*I think you can leave the arts, superior or inferior,
to the conscience of mankind.*

William Butler Yeats

These towering architectural shapes are very recognisable to Lake District lovers as part of Honister Pass, with the sunshine patterns playing on the slopes of Fleetwith Pike in Borrowdale. The grey slate rocks contrasts well against the grassland which is nearly always yellow at that height surrounded by rust coloured brackens, and parts of the old slate mine roofs can be seen as you glance down the valley.

This point is reached along the B5289 which connects Borrowdale and Buttermere, and as you travel along, distant views of the fells of Pillar and Great Gable can be seen, also Crummock Water and Loweswater. This area was commercially mined for its fine green slate since the 1750s. Quarrying stopped in 1986 but reopened again in 1997.

66. Honister Pass and Fleetwith Pike in Borrowdale.

Honister Pass Borrowdale
Wendy M Stewart

Advice is like snow - the softer it falls, the longer it dwells upon, and the deeper in sinks into the mind.

Samuel Taylor Coleridge

Even in the winter whiteness of heavy snowfalls that obliterate the landscape, there is colour and pattern in the view. The winding fence follows a farm road creating a linear design into the picture, leading past an out-building and on towards the small hamlet of Hartsop, just north of Kirkstone. This view was painted at Crookabeck, a working farm run by my cousins, whom I visited some years ago during a very cold spring. I sat on the window seat of this beautiful seventeenth century farmhouse in Patterdale, which straddles a small track to Hartsop, to study this picturesque setting.

Crookabeck nestles under Place Fell, with a range of fells including Helvellyn, St Sunday Crag, Fairfield and many others just a short distance away. Brotherswater is also just a short walk from the farm. Times have changed now for, while still a busy farm with Herdwick sheep and Angora goats, whose products can be bought from the farm shop, it also now offers luxury bed and breakfast accommodation.

67. Sitting in Crookabeck Farm, Patterdale, facing Hartsop Dodd.

Art is a harmony parallel with nature.　　　　　　　　　Paul Cezanne

Derwentwater and its surrounding panoramic views can be appreciated from every angle, and when I travelled along the eastern road past the lake of Derwentwater on the B5289, I glanced back from my original starting point of Keswick, and saw the giant of Skiddaw towering over the view, with all its majesty and snow covered tops. The late autumn colours of the trees and brackens further enhanced the view on this windless day, and soon my sketch was finished in my little book for posterity.

Skiddaw, towering over Derwentwater, is edged to the west by the A591 to Bassenthwaite, and is the fourth highest mountain in England at over 3000 feet high. To the east stands Blencathra, also known as Saddleback, and when at the top, the Isle of Man can be seen 60 miles away, and also, on a clear day the Mourne Mountains in Ireland, a distance of 120 miles.

Skiddaw is made up from some of the oldest rocks in the Lake District, with soft shale formed from marine deposits, creating the unique Skiddaw Slate. Some of this slate resonated with musical notes, and in the 1780s Peter Crossthwaite collected and shaped enough musical stones to be able to play them for concerts. This idea was taken a step further in the 1830s when Joseph Richardson played the Skiddaw Musical Stones at a command performance of his improved set to Queen Victoria. They are now in the Keswick Museum. Today a group of musicians have revived this music and in 2005 set up a series of concerts, and so the musical stones continue.

68. Looking north at Skiddaw and Derwentwater.

Look back, and smile on perils past.   Sir Walter Scott

Wastwater was a good subject to paint with Yewbarrow on my left, and Scafell, Great Gable and Lingmell much in evidence further away, so I sat on my little stool to paint. After a little while, the further end of the lake became shrouded in mist, but my foreground was lit up with the sunshine, so I left it that way to show the rapidly changing weather conditions that had occurred. The blues of Yewbarrow became the dominant feature, whilst the desolate feeling of the foreground was captured with the browns and reds of the autumn tints, all painted with strong contrasting colours.

   Yewbarrow is on the north western flank of Wastwater, once known as Broadwater, a lake which is three miles long, one third of a mile wide and over 270 feet deep, and is indeed very cold. Fed by the River Irt, which flows out again, it then travels down to Ravenglass and into the Irish Sea. This spot is reached by travelling to Gosforth on the A595, then turning east to Netherwasdale.

69. Wastwater with Yewbarrow, Great Gable and Scafell.

Come forth into the light of things, let nature be your teacher.   William Wordsworth

Standing on the edge of Windermere in the bay at Low Wray, I watched the ducks endlessly chasing each other, and thought what an interesting curtain, or camouflage, the hanging branches made for spying upon the wildlife. This area is marked off with buoys to indicate a 'No-Go' area for any motor craft, thus giving the wildlife a more peaceful place for breeding, but sailing craft are permitted to anchor within this area. I have often taken that privilege and, because of its shallow depth, have anchored in safety when in the northern lake to make a meal, then sit and paint. I rowed ashore here to explore in an area called Pull Woods, and made a water sketch of these overhanging branches with the entrance to the bay in the distance beyond.

There is a National Trust campsite in this vicinity and also a very interesting 'Castle', built in the Gothic Revival Style in 1840, and worth going to see. Built for a retired Liverpool Surgeon, using his wife's fortune from the production of gin, he also built Wray Church, near to Wray Castle, which stands in 65 acres of beautiful parkland. He died at 96 in 1875, leaving the estate to his nephew, Preston Rawnsley, whose cousin, Hardwick Rawnsley, became vicar of Wray Church. He was also one of the founders of the National Trust, for he had strong views on the preservation of the landscape.

Beatrix Potter's wealthy parents rented the castle when she was sixteen in 1882 for holidays, where she was much influenced by Hardwick's views, and eventually used her fortune from her books to buy up many acres of the land in that area; she bought her home named Hilltop in 1905.

70. Through the trees at Pull Wood, Low Wray Bay.

I gazed - and gazed - but little thought
What wealth the show to me had brought   William Wordsworth

Viewing Windermere on a late autumn day from the shelter of the Lake District Boat Club to which I have belonged for years, I realize that the colours and look of the place change in so many subtle ways according to the seasons, that for every day there is a different scene to view, and by late autumn it needs softer warm colours, in ranges of greys and browns. As my starting point for sailing, I never tired of reviewing this panoramic scene, and made many pictures from this point. Founded in 1965, it is a family inspired club to promote water activities, what one could say as 'Messing about in boats!' From this vantage point one can see the large old steamers passing by, plying their trade from one end of the lake to the other.

This place is on the shore of Bowness Bay. The town is more accurately called Bowness-on-Windermere, and is about three miles from the town of Windermere, an area gaining this name because of the railway halt arriving in 1847 at the village of Birthwaite, the nearest that it could be built to the lake. The two towns are now joined with a ribbon development of Victorian buildings. Many fine residences of rich industrialists of that era are dotted around the lake, such as Storrs Hall, Langdale Chaise, Brockholes, and in Bowness can be found The Belsfield, now a hotel, home in the late 1800s of the wealthy chairman of the Barrow steelworks, Henry Schneider.

The earliest reference to Bowness to be found was for 1190, with the place being called *Bulenas,* meaning Bullheadland. The name of Windermere is derived from the Old Norse *Onundar Myrr*, and in the eighteenth century it was often referred to as Windander.

71. Windermere from Bowness Bay, in the autumn.

Fill your paper with the breathings of your heart.   William Wordsworth

This painting of the fir trees, standing in deep snow, could be anywhere, but was inspired by walking in the Grisedale forest near Slatterthwaite, a small village approximately four miles south of Hawkshead. There they stood, regally clothed with snow in the still air, after a new fall of snow, stark against the glare and whiteness of the surrounding land. I shook a small tree nearby to watch the fine powdery snow fall gently to the ground, making it now bare of dressing which then became the darkest focal point in my vision. Some winter bird was rustling in the bare undergrowth of one tree, not caring to tread onto the snow, but perhaps searching for a winter meal.

I kept this image in my mind, and tried to reproduce this scene accurately after I had thawed out later in the day, needing very few colours to recreate the feeling of being alone in the snow-covered wilderness.

Many places in the Lake District have conifers planted, and there are a lot of varieties, such as pines, larches, firs, spruce, cedars, hemlocks and yews, although generally speaking, people erroneously refer to most of them as firs. Ancient species have been found in fossils dating back to 300 million years ago, growing as far north as the Arctic Circle. They are survivors in low temperatures, because their winter adaptation alters their biochemistry for withstanding the extreme cold. Some species of fir trees grow from 30 to 260 feet high and part of their economic value is for the timber and paper making industries. Pines were used extensively for pit props in the mines, found all over the Lake District, because these trees tend to grow tall and straight.

72. The hills clothed in winter garb near Slatterthwaite.

Art is not what you see, but what you make others see.   Edgar Degas

From all angles this small hamlet of Watendlath is a painter's paradise. At every angle of this secluded spot is another view, for making a sketch worth attempting, and I wandered down to a vantage point below the little bridge to look back at the buildings. I had a fine view of the hills beyond, surrounding the lake and studied the buildings nestling amongst the mixed trees beside the deep blue tarn. I made my painting of the packhorse bridge, as traditionally made as the old farmhouse, where the hefted Herdwick sheep are still farmed.

The name Watendlath is derived from the Old Norse word *vatn-endi-nlaoa*, which means 'water end barn'. It was once owned by Furness Abbey, as was much of the land hereabouts, and was also featured in a book by Sir Hugh Walpole (1884-1941) titled *Judeth Paris*, one of the *Rogue Herries* series. This seven acre tarn, which is teeming with brown and rainbow trout, was given to the National Trust by Princess Louise, Queen Victoria's daughter, in memory of her brother, King Edward VII. This is still a working farm, offering bed and breakfast and also a tea room for the tired walkers, who brave the distances over the fells.

73. The hamlet of Watendlath near Derwentwater.

WATENDLATH
NR . DERWENTWATER .

Walk while ye have the light, lest darkness come upon you.　　　John Ruskin

It is amazing what can be done with a minimum of equipment when pushed for an answer, and when I made this sketch I had no paintbox with me when I stopped on the road side, having travelled south from Caldbeck, and skirted the fells towards Mungrisedale. However, I had three tubes of water-paint, my drinking water, and my sketch book, with a brush lodged in its pages. Paynes grey, light red and raw sienna were the tubes in my pocket, together with a non-waterproof pen. I used the lid of my sandwich box, fashioned a small water-holder out of a piece of silver foil that held my food, and I was in business again!

　　I faced Stone Ends Farm across the fields, a mist rising slightly, giving the whole scene an eerie, surreal feel to it. Heavy clouds rolled by, revealing again the warm colours behind them. This hasty painting, quickly drawn into the wet paint with a pen, now reminds me of the luminous pink glow I looked upon, and the pleasure I had that week roaming over those fells.

　　From the south, this area can be reached from the A66, turning at Scales towards Mungrisedale, and taking the high road past Carrock Fell to Caldbeck, or reverse this route from the north.

74. Mists rising on the fells above Mungrisedale.

Nothing ever becomes real till it is experienced.   John Keats

When driving north along the A591 past Thirlmere, the road eventually rises at the end of the lake and curves down into the Vale of St. John. I am not sure whether this name applies to this beautiful valley in total, but the view as one enters this area is unexpectedly spectacular, so I returned to the car park I had just passed to leave the car, and walked along till I found the spot that I wished to paint. The view had all the hallmarks of an ideal composition, the meandering road, strong foreground with farms and fields, and distant hills to draw one's eye through to the promise of further explorations. That road led on to Keswick, a few miles further north.

The landscape of this vale, unchanged over time, is scattered with small farms, and disused quarries from the old mining works. St Johns Beck meanders through the bottom of this valley, being the outflow water from Thirlmere. The earliest church of St John dates from 1554, but the present one of 1845 incorporates parts of the original, and a place not easy to find. The single track road that passes it, was once an important road From Matterdale to Wanthwaite.

75. St. John in the Vale, near Thirlmere looking north.

Sunshine is delicious, rain is refreshing, wind braces us up, snow is exhilarating; there is really no such thing as bad weather, only different kinds of good weather.   John Ruskin

This painting incorporated much of what made this composition interesting by chance. Peering down at Derwentwater with Blencathra towering in the background, the blue sky delineated the white snow covered mountain, and was reflected on the surface of Derwentwater, flanked by autumn trees and short clipped grass manicured by the local sheep. Autumn is a special time for making water sketches, for the green colours of summer change to different shades of yellows, reds, browns, and purples from the grasses, brackens and heathers.

　　Whatever the weather, you can see this point of view by travelling along the western route, high above Derwentwater towards Swinside. Although a beautiful area in which to roam, this area is covered with bracken, and the chances of picking up sheep ticks onto you or your dog are great, for they live in the upper parts of the bracken and readily attach themselves to anything that brushes past, and our uplands are well covered with both. The greatest threat from ticks is that they are carriers of Lime disease, so prevention of infection is essential with the right clothing, medication and vigilance.

76. Blencathra as seen across Derwentwater.

In the late summer when the grasses were turning yellow and the brackens orange, I found myself looking down upon Rydal Water from a good vantage point. This lake is so sheltered from any winds at times that on this occasion it almost appeared to be a mirror, reflecting the deep blue summer sky, surrounded by the dried out grasses on Loughrigg Fell. I made my sketch to capture the contrasting colours of this little lake in its peaceful landscape.

Rydal Water lies in an east-west direction and from end to end is only three quarters of a mile long and is in the vale of Rothay, which was formed by glacial action. The river Rothay runs down the length of it, travelling through Rydal Water from Grasmere and down to the shores of Windermere. This was once called Rowthemere or Rothaymere, and the southern part is leased to the National Trust.

There are two little islands on RydalWater, Heron Isle and Little Isle, which is a mere nineteen yards long. Heron Isle is sometimes used as a refuge by the red deer, who swim across from White Moss Common. There are many waterfowl here including coots, great crested grebes, swans and red breasted mergansers, and a large population of fish is to be found underwater - and so are the anglers ashore.

77. The calm of Rydal Water surrounded by Loughrigg Fell.

Rydal Water

I found this corner by chance in Grasmere, for I wandered up the road opposite the church, and came to the end of the houses in the trees. At that point I went through a gate and strolled to the water's edge, where there was a convenient seat hidden in the undergrowth. I studied the effects of the onset of autumn amongst the banks of trees, (mainly deciduous) on the opposite shore, showing almost pink and mauve tints. The further away the trees were, the more the falling mists hid the view of them, and brought into closer relief the little boathouse and immediate trees beside it. I can almost still smell the wood smoke of the autumn fires there.

Grasmere is well known for its famous sports day in August, first held in 1852, and having contests in Cumberland wrestling, fell running and hound trailing amongst the foremost activities. The churchyard has the graves of William Wordsworth and his family, for he lived round here from 1799 to 1850 when he died.

From Grasmere the A591 leading north to Keswick goes up the Dunmail Raise. Earlier in my lifetime, this was an extremely steep road through the mountains, but has since been somewhat flattened and straightened. Dunmail was the last Celtic King of Cumbria who was defeated by the Anglo Saxons in 945 AD. The name of Grasmere could possibly come from the Old Norse words either *griss* = little pig, or *grise* = lush green vegetation, because it is known that Old Norse was the Cumbrian language well into the thirteenth century and the dialect is still based on Norse. Therefore Grasmere could mean the lake of swine.

78. A corner of Grasmere.

I am following Nature without being able to grasp her.   Claude Monet

This sketch of a farmhouse in the autumn sunshine, highlights all that is appealing in this area for painting. The changing season from summer to autumn produces a fine array of colour, and on a sunny day with clouds creating shadows that float across the mountain tops, produce a variety of patterns to study. The colourful trees before they have lost their autumn leaves act as a foil to the grey farmhouse that is dwarfed by the fells beyond. Happily I worked on this view and speedily made my sketch before the light had changed.

The Langdale valley is very long and narrow, with the Great Langdale Beck running through it. The valley bottom is scattered with small buildings and farmhouses, and there is also a campsite for visitors who venture this far. The road eventually leads up a winding road and on into the Little Langdale valley.

This area is a delight to thousands, for here is the start from the Old Dungeon Ghyll Inn for many climbers into the surrounding Cumbrian mountains, where Bowfell, Raven Crag and Scafell Pike (3209 feet), the highest mountain in England, are to be found. Also above the inn is Stickle Tarn, from which Mill Beck cascades past the inn. It was originally a farm and an inn, which was named Middlefell Inn in some records of 1885, and then became Dalehead Inn. Dungeon Ghyll is the Old Norse term for a 'stream flowing through a dark place.'

79. An autumn scene of a farmhouse in the Langdales.

Examine nature accurately, but write from recollection, and trust more to the imagination than the memory.
                                                                    Samuel Taylor Coleridge

Kirkstone Pass is the highest pass that is open for motor traffic in England and when you reach the top this fact can be seen, for the view is so vast it is past belief! Travelling on the A592 over this pass, it connects Ambleside in the south, to Patterdale in the north. I walked above the Kirkstone Inn to do this water sketch, facing the northern hills, Brothers Water and beyond, Ullswater.

At this height the grasses rarely looked very green, and the fell sides were dotted about with various sizes of rocks, or perhaps they were distant sheep? I perched by a small creek, with clear, running water to finish my work and wrapped my coat closer, for the wind was sneaking through my outer layers of clothing. I could just see Brothers Water glistening in the distance and catching the sunlight.

There are records dating back to 1496 of the foundations of the Kirkstone Inn being previously of a 15th century monastery, and this is very believable, because this site has been an important Coaching Inn on the road connecting the two valleys for many years. Coachmen used to ask passengers to walk up the hills for the sake of the horses, who might manage with great effort the coach, but not a full load. There is a large standing stone about 650 yards from the Kirkstone Inn along the Ullswater road, that has the shape of a church, and it is believed that this Kirk stone name came from the Old Norse word Kyrka = church.

80. Kirkstone Pass, looking north.

I have believed the best of every man. And find that to believe is enough to make a bad man show him at his best, or even a good man swings his lantern higher.   William Butler Yeats

This view of Catbells, the mountain seen from across Derwentwater, was painted to capture the strong patterns and colour highlighted by the sunshine. At the right time of day it is a most dramatic view, and did not take many colours to illustrate this well known point, painted from the eastern shore on Derwentwater near Friars Crag, which is a promontory of rocks, now with a seat at its tip, and well beloved by the viewing public.

Catbells is 1,480 feet high, and lies two miles south of Keswick overlooking the western side of Derwentwater. Parts of it in Yewthwaite Comb are covered with the spoil heaps and mineshafts from old lead mines, that operated there from about 1849. The Yewthwaite Mine had a brief life, and closed finally in 1893, probably not being able to compete economically with the other mines situated nearer to Keswick. All the shafts have been closed off or filled now. It is one of the most sought-after fells to climb, not having too great a height or gradient to climb, and popular with families.

81. Derwentwater, with Catbells ahead.

Don't be an art critic. Paint. There lies salvation.   Samuel Taylor Coleridge

At the far end of Wasdale there is a magical area, with sheltered fields and streams fit for a fairy kingdom. I sat there on a boulder, to paint my view of Great Gable, purple with heathers and turning pink with bracken. The late summer ensured that the fields were by now various shades of yellow, as the cool waters of the brook bustled along amongst the stones, stirring one's nose with mountain fragrances. A fisherman had taken up his position next to the stream, with rod, sandwiches and his thoughts for company, whilst I tried to capture the scene in my little book.

This point is right in the middle of the Cumbrian range of mountains, with Seatallan, Haycock, Pillar, Kirk Fell, Great Gable, Great End, Bow Fell, Scafell Pike and Scafell arranged right round this valley. At the head of Wastwater, with the source of the River Irt and tributaries flowing past from the mountains, you can see the foothills of the nearest, and the top of Great Gable being caressed by the clouds.

Being in the centre of climbing activities, it was here that the Fell and Rock Climbing Club was formed in 1907 at the Wastwater Hotel by a group of like minded climbers, the first president being the famous climber Ashley Abraham, and included members who were some of the best British climbers who took part in the Everest and Himalayan Expeditions, including Sir John Hunt, Mike Westmacott, Alf Gregory, Sir Charles Evans, Chris Bonnington and Ian Clough to name just a few.

82. Great Gable and Lingmell Beck in Wasdale.

Don't be afraid in nature: one must be bold, at the risk of having been deceived and making mistakes.
                                                                    Camille Pissarro

This little water sketch of Lanty Tarn was a hasty one, produced between the frequent showers, which acted as a reminder to me for a further painting later. It captured the layout and colours of what I was looking at, and was sufficient for its task. It was a late summer view when the brackens were turning red and the leaves becoming yellow, with the mauve hills behind but I found that I had no time for further embellishments. This place is in a depression near the top of Keldas, to the west of Ullswater, and had a 'Picturesque' feel to it, being far from the 'tourist' areas.

    Lanty Tarn was named after Lancelot (Lanty) Dobson, whose family owned much of Grisedale in the eighteenth century, and all lived there in a great house near Grassthwaite Howe. It was then sold to the Marshall family living at Patterdale Hall, who enlarged the tarn and dammed it at one end to improve the fishing for himself, as well as for the locals. He built an ice house there, packed with straw and sawdust for keeping the caught fish fresh.

    If you stroll up there, you must stick to the path because it is all private land. Having climbed up from Glenridding at the southern end of Ullswater, from this point one can see over the landscape that surrounds this lake.

83. Lanty Tarn in Grisedale.

LANTY TARN, IN GRISDALE.

Natural abilities can almost compensate for the want of every kind of cultivation, but no cultivation of the mind can make up for the want of natural abilities.   John Ruskin

Whilst exploring the Western Fells of the Lake District I came across a packhorse bridge in a picturesque setting. Thankfully the weather was fine enough to make a small painting of it, highlighting the fells behind.

The Lake District probably has the largest collection of stone pack-horse bridges to be found in the world. During the period between 1650 and 1750 most were built, using local stones. A pack-horse bridge has a simple arch construction, narrow width and low walling suitable for the strings of horses with their loads of goods for sale from the Lake District to pass over unimpeded.

Wasdale Head is a small agricultural village in the National Park. The village claims to be home of the highest mountain (Scafell Pike), deepest lake (Wastwater), and the smallest church in England, and is at the 'head' of the valley of Wasdale, surrounded by some of England's highest mountains: Scafell Pike, Great Gable, Kirk Fell and Pillar, and is the recognised starting point for the ascent of Scafell Pike, and other peaks.

In this village the serious climbers gather. Their Fell and Rock Climbing Club produced a definitive Guide to Rock Climbing in the Lake District, which is much referred to when describing the ascents. These are graded according to the technical difficulty, strength needed, and severity of the climbs, from moderate (M), very difficult (VD), hard VD (HVD), mild or hard severe (MS or HS), mild very severe (MVS), very and hard very severe (VS and HVS) through to the extremely severe having its own grades (E1-10).

84. The Packhorse Bridge, Wasdale Head.

A thing of beauty is a joy forever: its loveliness increases;
it will never pass into nothingness.   John Keats

This hidden lake was a real find early in the morning, when the sun had not yet quite filled the sky with warmth and sunshine, leaving the mists still to clothe the landscape with softness and blurred edges. The sounds of the wildfowl scuttling in the reeds proved that there were creatures bent on securing food, whilst the black coots led out their young for an early jaunt. At this moment the spiders' webs were bedecked with droplets of water like shining necklaces, strung out between tall reeds, soon to be disturbed by the wind or by water fowl, or the swans on patrol. My little water sketch did not do justice to this scene, but when I now look upon it, I am reminded of the early morning scents of mist and trees and a nearby wood-smoke fire.

Elterwater is in the Langdale valley. Starting from Skelwith Bridge on the A593, one then branches off on the B5343 aiming towards the village of Elterwater beyond the lake itself. In the past, this area was important for quarrying Kirkstone green slate, but also there was a gunpowder works here, powered by great water-wheels in the River Brathay, which ran from 1824 until the 1930s with a large local workforce. The many workers cottages to be seen are now used for holiday lets. Herdwick sheep are farmed in this valley, the hardiest breed for this mountainous region.

The name of Elterwater is derived from the Old Norse word *elter* meaning swan. These aggressive birds, whooper swans, breed in Iceland, migrate yearly to the north of England, and regularly use Elterwater for their summer pasture. It is a shallow lake, offering aquatic plants and grasses for feeding upon, and when migrating, the swans often take fourteen to fifteen hours from Iceland, at speeds of up to 50 mph. The World Wildlife Trust rings many swans, and attach radio transmitters to track their behaviour, so they may learn more about them.

85. Elterwater on a calm morning.

Don't be afraid in nature: one must be bold,
at the risk of having been deceived and making mistakes.   Camille Pissarro

On my way back from my walk to the Tilberthwaite mining area I spotted this double bridge amid the autumn grasses. This bridge was on a packhorse route in the seventeenth century connecting the slate quarries in Hodge Close and Tilberthwaite to the hamlet of Little Langdale where the quarrymen lived. It straddles the River Brathay which flows from Little Langdale Tarn down to Elterwater, and thence to Windermere. I wanted to make a record of this bridge in my little book, but as it was spitting with rain, I propped myself up under my brolly and proceeded to do my best, finishing it off hastily when the drizzle became a downpour.

    Historically Little Langdale was at the intersection of several packhorse routes and was also the home of the notorious nineteenth century smuggler Lanty (Lancelot) Slee, who operated illegal stills hidden in local caves and quarries for making moonshine liquor, and another in a cave in Moss Rigg Quarry. He was born in 1800, of Irish descent, and outwardly was a wealthy farmer who built Greenback Farm in the valley in 1840, but stealthily sold moonshine whisky to the poor and rich alike, sending it over Wrynose and Hardknott Pass to Ravenglass on the packhorse route, for further distribution, making his fortune even larger. Convicted a couple of times and fined £150, he continued his trade until he died at the age of 78. One of his two sons lived until he was over 100 years old.

86. Slater Bridge across the River Brathay, Little Langdale.

The animation of the canvas is one of the hardest problems of painting.   Alfred Sisley

Winter seems to appear earlier the further north and the wilder the terrain. One autumn I drove past Grange with its double bridges, and kept straight on the B5289 to the end of Borrowdale, turning off to the left and up into the Borrowdale Fells where I found Stonethwaite, an isolated hamlet. It did have a local inn, and having obtained refreshment, I set out from there to explore the small but powerful stream hastening down the valley. This is Langstrath Beck in Borrowdale.

The timelessness and continuity of these mountain streams make me ponder about the limited span of our lives, and how best we should use it. I wished to record my scene, so chose a position that would best illustrate the bleakness of the place. Windy, wet, and cold though it was, I saw the beauty of this view, and I thought of the poem, *The Brook* by Alfred Lord Tennyson. As there are thirteen verses of this beautiful and evocative poem, I shall choose only four:

I come from haunts of coot and hern,*
And make a sudden sally,
And sparkle out among the fern,
To bicker down the valley.

By thirty hills I hurry down,
Or slip between the ridges,
By twenty thorps, a little town
And half a hundred bridges.

I chatter over stony ways
In little sharps and trebles,
I bubble into eddying bays,
I babble on the pebbles.

I chatter, chatter as I flow,
To join the brimming river,
For men may come and men may go,
But I go on for ever.

87. Langstrath Beck in Borrowdale.

*Hern comes from *hragra* (O.E.) for heron.

All great art is the work of the whole living creature, body and soul,
and chiefly of the soul.   John Ruskin

White Moss Common is a small area just over four and a half miles across, bounded on almost three sides within the curve of the A591 through from Windermere to Ambleside and situated by Rydal Water. It has its own miniature landscape, and as I stood approximately at its minor summit of about 400 feet, I could admire Rydal Water below me and the views beyond.

   I perched on one of the low crags, keeping my feet out of the boggy water that was running amongst the grasses, and recorded the colours of the purple hills, the grey crags, yellow and orange grasses and brackens, with the deep hues of the fir trees interspersed with the delicate birch trees.

   It is an area of contrasts, in the shadow of Nab Scar, with its rocky outcrops like petite mountains, where the area is crossed with many pathways leading through groves of trees. William Wordsworth walked up here when he lived locally in Dove Cottage in Rydal (from 1802 to 1813) and would skate on the small tarn, hidden on the common, that regularly froze over, thus it was known as Skaters Tarn. Having become overgrown with weeds and rhododendrons, the National Trust is now clearing it all out again.

88. White Moss Common, above Rydal Water.

Acknowledgements

I would like to thank the producers of, and acknowledge the inspiration derived from, the many Lakeland photographic and guide books I have collected over the years. These have fuelled my curiosity, and prompted me to search my maps to find some of the places depicted, and visit them, thus resulting in many hours of painting at these scenes. Amongst these books I must include:

The Lake District, C. H. D. Ackland; *Exploring the Lakes and Low Fells*, Bill Birkett; *Memories of the Lake District*, J Salmon, (publisher); *Lakeland High Tarns*, John Drews; *The Lake District,* John Curtis; *Lakeland Views* Val Corbett; *Lake District* D. W. Jones and A. E. Bowness; *Borrowdale*, M. Pearson, R. Warner and A. Pearson.

Lastly, but not least, I would like to thank my husband, Edward Murphy, for being patient with me, and the tolerance of my friends, when working long hours to complete this book. I would also like to thank the writers of other guide books, history books and publications that have guided me over the years, but are now lost, and any others that I have inadvertently not mentioned. And, of course, I must thank the poets and painters, from whom I have taken many of the quotations, many of whom appreciated the great outdoors as inspiration for their work.

Samuel Taylor Coleridge, 1772-1834
John Keats, 1795-1821
Rudyard Kipling, 1865-1936
Beatrix Potter, 1866-1943
John Ruskin, 1819-1900
Robert Southey, 1774-1843
Thomas de Quincey, 1785-1859
Christina Rossetti, 1830-1894
Sir Walter Scott, 1771-1832
Alfred Lord Tennyson, 1809-1892
William Wordsworth, 1770-1850
William Butler Yeats, 1865-1939

Paul Cezanne, 1839-1906
Edgar Degas, 1834-1917
Robert Delaunay, 1885-1941
Edouard Manet, 1832-1883
Claude Monet, 1840-1926
Camille Pissarro, 1830-1903
Pierre-Auguste Renoir, 1841-1919
Sir Joshua Reynolds, 1723-1792
Alfred Sisley, 1839-1899
Leonardo da Vinci, 1452-1519